Table of Contents

Go Boho,
page 7

Casual Saturday,
page 24

Holiday Flair,
page 43

Summer Fun,
page 10

Sew Trendy Fashions & Accessories for 18" Dolls

The popularity of the 18-inch doll is due in large part, I believe, to the fact that young girls can identify with them. They are made to look like modern girls. Some companies offer many choices, so you can buy a doll that truly resembles its owner. And with a little imagination (and young girls have loads of that), the doll can have a personality and a "life" with activities, friends, school, celebrations and chores—just like her proud owner. But to really make the connection, the dolls need clothes and accessories that appeal to the girls—contemporary styles, colors and fabrics with a little bling here and there. So that is what I have tried to do in this book—give you many choices for current designs to make a doll's wardrobe that reflects its owner's sense of style.

The fabrics and colors are suggestions. You can create many great outfits from the patterns in this book by mixing the separates and by using a variety of fabrics, colors and embellishments. I hope you enjoy making these designs your very own!

Meet the Designer

Chris Malone has been sewing and crafting most of her life and became an avid quilter about 15 years ago. She has had hundreds of designs published in industry magazines and books and authored several of her own. Recent book publications include *Pot Holders, Pinchers & More* and *Hooded Scarves & Gloves*. She resides in the beautiful state of Oregon.

General Instructions

Basic Sewing Supplies & Tools
- Sewing machine in good working order, preferably with zigzag stitch capability
- Good-quality all-purpose thread to match fabrics
- Sharp scissors and pinking shears
- Straight pins and hand-sewing needles
- Measuring tools
- Air- or water-soluble marking pens
- Steam iron, ironing board, pressing cloth and pressing ham (or use rolled-up washcloth)
- Permanent fabric adhesive (washable)

Optional
- Rotary cutter, mat and rulers
- Serger
- Tube-turning tool
- Elastic lacer

Fabric Selection
Knits are very popular now for clothing, so a number of the designs in this book feature knit fabrics. They are easy to cut and sew and most do not need a seam finish.

Small contemporary prints are most widely available in woven cottons. Keep scale in mind when selecting a print—use smaller scale prints for these small garments. Many of the designs call for a fat quarter of fabric, which is simply a precut 18 x 21-inch rectangle found in fabric stores, often displayed with a number of coordinating fabrics, making it a breeze to select a coordinated look.

Straight of Grain
Straight-of-grain arrows are given on most pattern pieces. Pieces with these arrows should be placed on the fabric with the arrow equal-distance from the selvage or finished edge of the fabric (Figure 1).

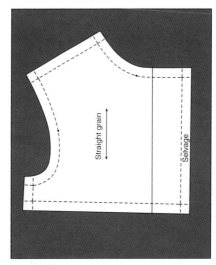

Figure 1

Fabrics With a Nap
Some fabrics have a raised surface called a nap. These fabrics feel different when rubbing your hand back and forth—with the nap feels smooth and against the nap feels rough. Fur, corduroy and velvet are fabrics with a nap.

When cutting fabric with a nap, pieces need to be cut with the nap going in the same direction. For example, each sleeve should be cut with the nap going in the same direction.

Knit fabrics stretch in all directions but more in some directions than others. Cut knits as if they had a nap with all pieces going in the same direction.

Faux fur can give a high-end look to your doll fashions. The following tips will make sewing with this specialty fabric easy.

- Position each pattern piece on the wrong side of the fabric and trace around pattern with a fabric marker.

- When cutting, use small scissors to make short clips on the fabric, keeping the point of the scissors close to the wrong side of the fabric. Go slowly so you clip as little of the fur as possible.

- Use a ballpoint needle to avoid puncturing the knit stitches of the fabric.

- The fur can be slippery. Use additional pins as necessary to hold pieces together.

- After stitching each seam, take the time to pull the fur from the seam. Run your fingers over the seam to loosen the fur from the seam. Use the blunt end of a seam ripper or a toothpick to pick fur from seam.

- Avoid ironing the fur. It may melt. If pressing is needed, use a cool iron and press on the wrong side of the fabric.

Construction Tips

How to Use the Patterns: To use the patterns in the book, trace pieces onto tissue paper, cut apart and pin tissue to fabric. Cut out on pattern lines, cutting through tissue and fabric. Alternately, you can copy patterns onto cardstock, cut out and trace around the patterns onto the fabric with a pencil or an air- or water-soluble pen. Be sure to transfer any necessary markings. Also, many instructions say to "Cut 2 from fabric, reverse 1." If your fabric is folded in half, with wrong sides together or right sides together, your one cut will automatically give you both pieces. Otherwise, just flip the pattern over for your second cut.

Seam Finishes: Seam finishes are only mentioned in the instructions when a particular finish is called for. Some of the fabrics, such as denim, are too bulky to fold under for a doubled hem, so the edges are zigzag-stitched or serged to eliminate a fold. Please feel free to finish seams as desired—serging,

zigzag-stitching, using pinking shears or even applying seam sealant. Some fabrics, such as knits and faux suede, do not require any seam finish.

Fasteners: Most of the garments in this book have snap sets for fasteners. The male half of the snap is sewn to the inside of the garment on the right side. The female half is sewn to the outside of the garment on the left side, so the right overlaps the left when closed. If you prefer, substitute hook-and-loop tape strips for the snaps.

Hems and Casings: The garments in the book all have either a single-fold or a double-fold hem. Individual instructions will specify the width of the folds. Measure and press the first fold. If it is a double hem, fold again, measuring from the folded edge. Edgestitch close to the final fold to finish. The same technique is true for the casings that will hold elastic, but you will need to leave an opening to insert the elastic. The instructions will tell you where to leave an opening.

Gathering: Many of the garments in this book have gathered sleeves or skirts. To accomplish successful gathers, begin by making two rows of longer-than-normal stitches inside the normal seam allowance, leaving long thread tails at each end (Figure 2).

Figure 2

With right sides together, pin section to be gathered to the appropriate garment section at each end and at the center (Figure 3).

Figure 3

Pull the bobbin threads at one end to gather. When half of the gathered section fits straightedge length, secure bobbin threads by twisting around a pin (Figure 4). Repeat for the second half of the section. Pin securely along the seam line, adjusting gathers evenly.

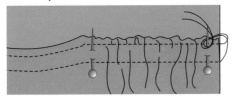

Figure 4

Stitch at seam line with gathered section on top and keeping gathers even so folds of fabric do not form while stitching (Figure 5). Remove gathering stitches after sewing seam.

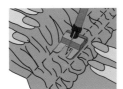

Figure 5

Creating Waistline Casing: Create a casing for elastic by pressing fabric to the wrong side as directed with individual pattern instructions. Press fabric to the wrong side, again as directed in the instructions with the pattern. Stitch close to the edge of the first fold line (Figure 6).

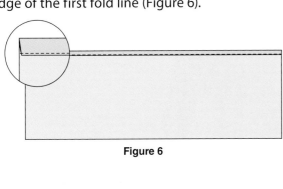

Figure 6

Thread the elastic through the casing using a safety pin or bodkin attached to one end of the elastic, making sure you don't pull the opposite end of the elastic all the way through the casing. Pin elastic even with the ends of the casing and stitch to secure in place (Figure 7).

Figure 7

Catch elastic ends in seams when completing the seams of the garment.

One Last Note Before You Begin

Please remember when making these doll clothes that the primary goal really is not to have a flawlessly constructed garment with every stitch in perfect alignment! It is more important to have a garment that is securely made so it can sustain the rigors of an enthusiastic costume change. Fasten each seam by using a backstitch at the starting and ending point and attach fasteners and embellishments securely. And, of course, choose fabrics and colors and embellishments that appeal to the girls who will be enjoying your creations! ∎

Go Boho

Call it retro or call it boho, this flowing skirt and peasant blouse will get your doll noticed. The braided cord can be used as a headband or belt.

Skirt & Blouse

Materials
- 3 coordinating fat quarters in colorful prints
- Fat quarter white-on-white dot
- Coordinating-color all-purpose thread
- 12 inches ¼-inch-wide elastic for blouse
- 11 inches ⅜-inch-wide elastic for skirt
- No. 8 or No. 16 orange pearl cotton, or embroidery floss
- Skein No. 3 dark brown pearl cotton
- 18 (5mm) wood beads
- Basic sewing supplies and equipment

Cutting
Use pattern templates H and I (page 49) for Go Boho blouse. Transfer pattern markings to fabric.

From 3 colorful prints:
- Cut one 6 x 14-inch strip for skirt top layer.
- Cut one 3½ x 21-inch strip for skirt middle layer.
- Cut two 3½ x 16½-inch strips for skirt bottom layer.

From white dot:
- Cut two blouse front/back (I) pieces on fold of fabric.
- Cut two sleeves (H) on fold of fabric.

Assembly
Stitch right sides together using a ¼-inch seam allowance, pressing seams open, unless otherwise directed.

Blouse
1. Sew sleeves to blouse front and back armholes (Figure 1).

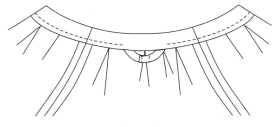

2. Press ¼-inch hem on neck edge (which includes top of sleeves). Fold an additional ⅜ inch to inside to form casing. Stitch close to edge, leaving a 1-inch opening for elastic.

3. Thread 12-inch length of ¼-inch-wide elastic through casing. Lap ends of elastic and stitch across to secure (Figure 2).

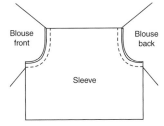

Figure 1

Figure 2

4. Sew opening in casing closed.

5. Sew front and back together at underarm seams, matching sleeve seams (Figure 3).

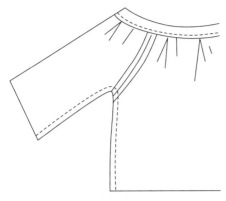

Figure 3

6. Press a doubled ¼-inch hem along bottom edge of blouse and bottom edge of each sleeve. Sew hem in place by hand using one strand of pearl cotton thread or two strands of embroidery floss or by machine.

Skirt

1. Press ½-inch hem to inside on one long edge of middle strip. Sew a row of gathering stitches ¼ inch from fold and a second line ⅜ inch from fold. Find the center of this strip and of the top layer strip and mark with pins.

2. Pull bobbin thread from one end to gather half of the strip. When this half is the same length as half of the top layer, tie off threads. Repeat with second half.

3. Overlap gathered edge of ruffle ½ inch onto skirt top, right sides up on both fabrics and matching centers. Distribute gathers evenly and pin (Figure 4). Sew layers together, stitching on top gathering line (¼ inch from fold). Remove bottom row of gathering stitches.

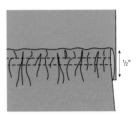

Figure 4

4. Sew the two strips for the bottom layer together along one short end to make a 3½ x 32-inch strip. Press and sew a ¼-inch double hem on one long edge of bottom strip.

5. Repeat steps 1–3, joining bottom ruffle to middle section.

6. Press a ¼-inch hem at the top edge of the skirt. Fold an additional ½–1 inch to inside and stitch close to edge to form casing.

7. Thread the 11-inch length of ⅜-inch-wide elastic through casing. Pin ends of elastic even with open ends of casing and stitch to secure (Figure 5).

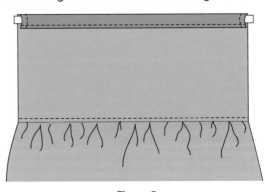

Figure 5

8. Sew center back seam to finish.

Belt

1. Cut six 32-inch lengths of brown pearl cotton. Measure 6 inches from one end and tie strands together into a knot.

2. Divide strands into three sets of 2 strands each and braid these sets together for 11 inches. Knot end to hold.

3. String three beads onto each 2-strand set on each end.

Tip

When braiding the skirt belt, pinning the knot to a sturdy surface helps hold it in place while braiding.

4. Tie a knot below the beads on each strand set, 3½–4½ inches from the braided section. Trim off strands to ½ inch below the beads.

5. If desired, apply a drop of no-fray solution to end of each strand. ■

Summer Fun

Get your doll ready for a fun summer picnic with this cool reversible blouse and shorts set, backpack and picnic blanket.

Blouse, Shorts, Backpack & Picnic Blanket

Materials

- Fat quarter tangerine broadcloth for shorts and blouse
- Fat quarter multicolored print for blouse
- Fat quarter turquoise broadcloth for backpack
- 9 x 18-inch piece of multicolored fleece for blanket
- 11 inches ⅜-inch-wide elastic for shorts
- 22 inches ¼-inch-wide elastic for blouse
- Coordinating-color all-purpose thread
- 14 x 6½-inch piece of lightweight (sewable) fusible web
- 18-inch piece black middy braid for backpack drawstrings
- Black cord stop for drawstrings
- Basic sewing supplies and equipment

Cutting

Use pattern templates E, F, G, H and I (pages 47–49) for Summer Fun. Transfer pattern markings to fabric.

From tangerine broadcloth:
- Cut two shorts backs (E), reversing one.
- Cut two shorts fronts (F), reversing one.
- Cut two shorts pockets (G), reversing one.
- Cut one 1¾ x 15½-inch strip for shorts waistband.
- Cut one blouse back (I) on fold, following cutting line for Summer Fun Back.

From multicolored print:
- Cut two sleeves (H) on fold, using cutting line for Summer Fun blouse.
- Cut one blouse front (I) on fold, using cutting line for Summer Fun Front.

From turquoise broadcloth:
- Cut one 2 x 20-inch strip for backpack straps.

Assembly

Stitch right sides together using a ¼-inch seam allowance, pressing seams open, unless otherwise directed.

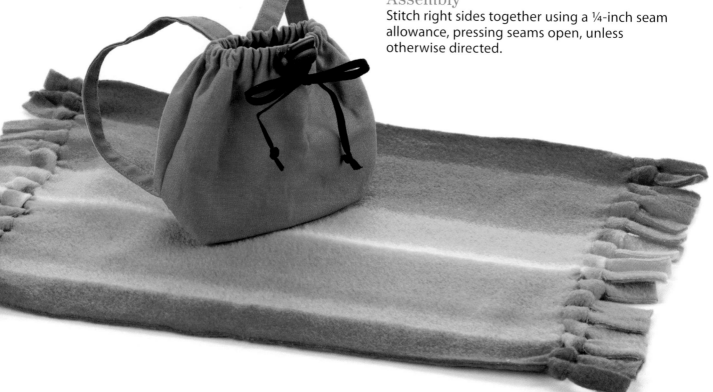

Shorts

1. Press slanted edge of each pocket ¼ inch to the wrong side; topstitch ⅛ inch from fold (Figure 1).

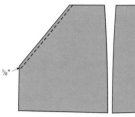

Figure 1

2. Press long side and bottom edges of pockets ¼ inch to wrong side. Place pockets on each shorts front, with top and short side edges even with top and sides of shorts. Topstitch ⅛ inch from folded edges to attach pockets (Figure 2).

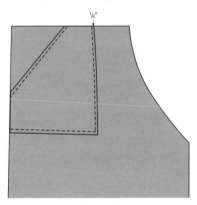

⅛"

Figure 2

3. Sew center front seam and center back seam.

4. Sew side seams (Figure 3).

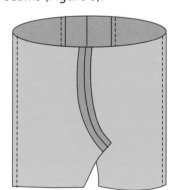

Figure 3

5. Join short ends of waistband. Fold waistband in half lengthwise, wrong sides together and press (Figure 4).

Figure 4

6. Unfold and press a ¼-inch hem on one long side of waistband. Sew remaining raw waistband edge to top of shorts, matching waistband seam to shorts center back seam (Figure 5).

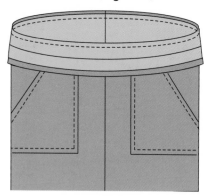

Figure 5

7. Fold waistband over to inside of shorts. Topstitch waistband, catching inside waistband edge in stitches. Leave a 1-inch opening in center back (Figure 6).

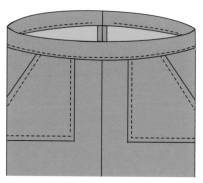

Figure 6

8. Thread the 11-inch length of ⅜-inch elastic into waistband casing through back opening. Overlap elastic ends and stitch across to secure (Figure 7).

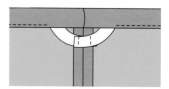

Figure 7

9. Stitch opening in the waistband closed.

10. Serge or zigzag-stitch lower edge of shorts. Press this edge ½ inch to the wrong side and stitch to hem.

11. Sew inner leg seam, matching center seams (Figure 8).

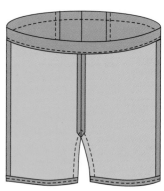

Figure 8

Reversible Blouse

1. Press ¼ inch to wrong side on lower edge of each sleeve. Fold over an additional ⅜ inch to form a casing on each sleeve; press. Stitch close to edge on each sleeve (Figure 9).

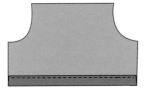

Figure 9

2. Cut two 5-inch-long pieces of ¼-inch-wide elastic. Thread elastic through casings; leave ends extending even with ends of casings. Stitch across ends to secure elastic pieces (Figure 10).

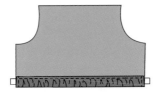

Figure 10

3. Sew sleeves to blouse front and back armholes (Figure 11).

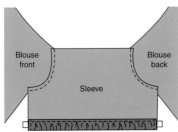

Figure 11

4. Press ¼ inch to the wrong side along neck edge (which includes top of sleeves). Fold over an additional ⅜ inch to form casing. Stitch close to the edge, leaving a 1-inch opening for the elastic.

5. Thread remaining 12-inch length of elastic into casing. Overlap elastic ends and stitch across to secure. Stitch opening in casing closed.

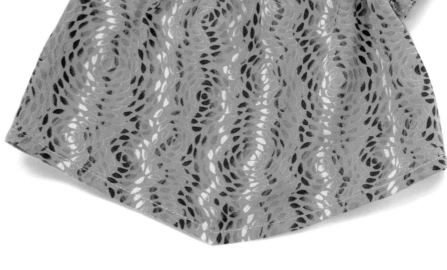

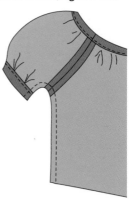

6. Sew blouse front and back together at underarm, matching sleeve seams (Figure 12).

Figure 12

7. Press and sew a doubled ¼-inch hem along bottom edge of blouse. ***Note:*** *The blouse is reversible by changing front and back. One side will be all multicolored print with an angled bottom edge; the reverse is tangerine with multicolored sleeves and a straight bottom.*

Backpack

1. Place fusible web, web side down, on wrong side of turquoise fabric in upper left corner. Follow manufacturer's directions to adhere web to fabric. Remove paper backing and fold fabric up and over making sure fold is at edge of web. Fuse the layers together. Cut two 6½ x 6-inch rectangles from fused portion of fabric.

2. Remove a 1-inch square from the bottom corners of each fused rectangle (Figure 13).

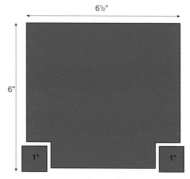

Figure 13

3. Stitch two ⅜-inch-long buttonholes in the center of one of the fused rectangles, starting ⅝ inch from top edge and making them ½ inch apart (Figure 14). **Note:** *This will be the front of the backpack.*

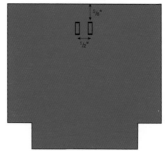

Figure 14

4. Pin and join the two rectangles on side and bottom edges (Figure 15).

Figure 15

5. To form bottom of bag, fold bottom seam up 1½ inches to match side seams and stitch across (Figure 16). Trim excess beyond ¼ inch.

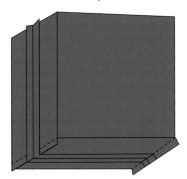

Figure 16

6. Turn bag right side out. Press a ½-inch casing to inside; stitch close to edge.

7. To make strap, press strip in half lengthwise, wrong sides together. Open strip up and press each long edge almost to centerfold line (Figure 17). Fold in ¼ inch on each short end. Fold strip back in half and topstitch all around, close to edge.

Figure 17

8. To attach strap, fold strap in half at an angle and stitch the folded section to bag back, just below casing stitching. Stitch across the folded end to hold (Figure 18).

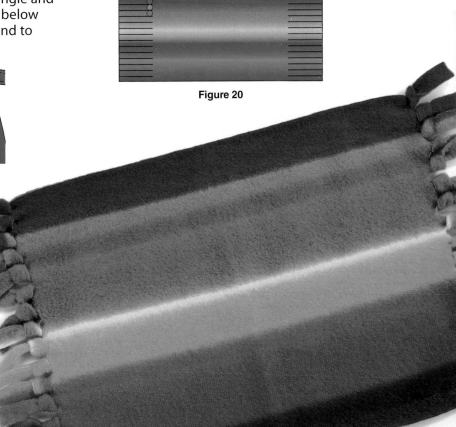

Figure 18

9. Bring strap ends down to bottom of bag, fold up 1 inch and pin to the back at an angle. Stitch ends securely in place (Figure 19).

Figure 19

10. Thread braid through backpack casing through buttonholes. Insert each end into a hole in the cord stop. Tie a knot in the ends of the braid and pull to close the backpack. Tie excess in a bow.

Blanket

1. Cut 3-inch-long slits, about ½ inch apart, on each 9-inch side of the fleece rectangle.

2. Tie a knot in each strip, close to the center section of the blanket (Figure 20). Trim ends even, if desired. ■

3"
½"

Figure 20

Sweet Dreams

Fuzzy slippers and a comfy pillow complete this cute pajama set. What else could a doll need?

Slippers, Pillow & Pajamas

Materials
- Scrap white felt
- Fat quarter white solid
- Fat quarter blue-and-green print
- ⅛ yard green dot
- ⅛ yard white Sherpa fur
- ⅓ yard knit star print
- ⅓ yard gray stretchy cotton knit
- Coordinating-color all-purpose thread
- 3 or 4 small snap sets
- 24 inches 1-inch-wide lightly gathered white lace
- 18 inches ⅛-inch-wide blue satin ribbon
- 11 inches ⅜-inch-wide elastic
- Fiberfill
- Permanent fabric adhesive
- Basic sewing supplies and equipment

Cutting
Use pattern templates J, K, L, M, N, O, P, Q and R (pages 50–53) for Sweet Dreams following cutting instructions for pajamas. Transfer pattern markings to fabric.

From scrap white felt:
- Cut two slipper bottom soles (P), reversing one.

From white solid:
- Cut one 5½ x 14½-inch rectangle for pillow.

From blue-and-green print:
- Cut one 7½ x 12-inch rectangle for pillowcase.

From green dot:
- Cut one 3¾ x 12-inch strip for pillowcase trim.

From white Sherpa fur:
- Cut two upper slipper pieces (Q), reversing one.
- Cut two upper slipper soles (R), reversing one.

From knit star print:
- Cut two top fronts (M), reversing one.
- Cut one top back (K) on fold.
- Cut one neck facing (N) on fold.
- Cut two sleeves (O), reversing one.

From gray stretchy cotton knit:
- Cut two leggings fronts (J), reversing one.
- Cut two leggings backs (L), reversing one.

From gathered white lace:
- Cut one 12-inch length and two 6-inch lengths.

Assembly
Stitch right sides together using a ¼-inch seam allowance, pressing seams open, unless otherwise directed.

Pajama Leggings
1. Follow steps 1–4 in instructions for the Back to School leggings (page 39).

2. Press a ¼-inch hem at lower edge of the leggings. Pin folded edge over top edge of a 6-inch length of lace. Topstitch ⅛ inch from fold, catching lace in stitches. Trim off any excess lace at the end. Repeat for second leg (Figure 1).

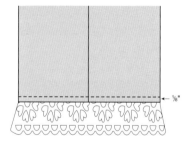

Figure 1

3. Follow steps 6 and 7 in the instructions for the Back to School leggings to finish the pajama leggings.

Pajama Top
1. Follow steps 1–10 in the instructions for the Back to School top (page 39) to construct the pajama top except that for the pajamas the side with snaps is the front. ***Note:*** *If desired, eliminate the top snap set and press the top corners back for a collared look.*

2. Tie a 6-inch length of ribbon into a bow and tack it to the pajama front.

Slippers

Note: *When sewing fur, make the seams look better by using the tip of your seam ripper or a large needle to pull some fur out of the seam.*

1. Fold and sew a ¼-inch hem on the slipper upper pieces (Figure 2).

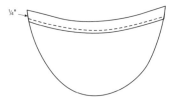

Figure 2

2. Sew the slipper upper pieces to the upper soles with right side of slipper upper against the wrong side of upper sole (Figure 3). Clip curves and turn right side out.

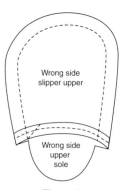

Wrong side slipper upper

Wrong side upper sole

Figure 3

3. Glue a felt sole to bottom of each slipper.

4. Tie two 6-inch lengths of ribbon into bows. Tack a bow to the top of each slipper.

Pillow & Pillowcase

1. Fold the white solid rectangle in half so it measures 5½ x 7¼ inches; sew all around, leaving a 3-inch opening on the short end (Figure 4). Trim corners and turn right side out to make the pillow form.

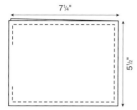

Figure 4

2. Fill the pillow form with fiberfill so pillow is full but not firm. Fold in seam allowance on the opening and hand- or machine-stitch the opening closed to finish.

3. To make pillowcase, pin the 12-inch length of lace to one long edge of the 3¾ x 12-inch green dot strip with right sides up (Figure 5). Baste in place.

Figure 5

4. Press a ¼-inch single hem to the wrong side on the other long edge.

5. Sew the blue-and-green print rectangle to the lace side of the green dot strip.

6. Fold the green dot strip in half lengthwise, wrong sides facing, so folded hem edge aligns with seam between the stitched pieces. Topstitch on the right side, catching green trim edge in stitches (Figure 6).

Figure 6

7. Fold pillowcase in half lengthwise with right sides together and sew the two raw edges together, matching seams (Figure 7).

Figure 7

8. Turn pillowcase right side out and insert pillow form. ■

Outrageous Ruffles

This fun, two-piece dress has a coordinating purse loaded with ruffles to make a complete outfit for your doll.

Two-Piece Dress Ensemble & Purse

Materials
- ⅛ yard green dot
- 1 fat quarter white solid (for bodice lining)
- ½ yard green floral print
- Coordinating-color all-purpose thread
- 11 inches ⅜-inch-wide elastic
- 3 small snap sets
- Permanent fabric adhesive
- Basic sewing supplies and equipment

Cutting
Use pattern templates for Outrageous Ruffles A, B, C and D (pages 46, 47). Transfer pattern markings to fabric.

From green dot:
- Cut two purse front/back (D) pieces.
- Cut two 1 x 6-inch strips for purse straps.
- Cut one 1½ x 10-inch strip, one 1½ x 10½-inch strip and one 1½ x 11-inch strip for ruffles.

From white solid:
- Cut 1 left back bodice (A) for lining.
- Cut 1 right back bodice (B) for lining.
- Cut 1 front bodice (C) for lining.

From floral print:
- Cut one left back bodice (A), right back bodice (B) and front bodice (C).
- Cut one 5 x 22-inch strip for bodice skirt.
- Cut one 8 x 22-inch strip for skirt.
- Cut two 2 x 8-inch strips for shoulder straps.
- Cut two purse front/back (D) pieces for lining.
- Cut two 1 x 6-inch strips for purse strap linings.

Assembly
Stitch right sides together using a ¼-inch seam allowance, pressing seams open, unless otherwise directed.

Two-Piece Dress Ensemble
1. Sew bodice front to right and left backs at side seams. Repeat with lining pieces.

2. To make shoulder straps, fold each strip in half lengthwise, right sides together. Stitch long edges together and across one short end (Figure 1). Trim corners and turn right side out; press.

Figure 1

3. Place raw edge of one strap at top of front bodice where indicated on pattern; baste. Repeat with second strap and right back bodice. Trim off strap corner to match bodice edge (Figure 2).

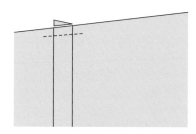

Figure 2

4. Pin stitched bodice and lining units with right sides facing, and sew neck and back edge and armholes—do not sew across shoulder seam (Figure 3). Clip curves and turn right side out; press.

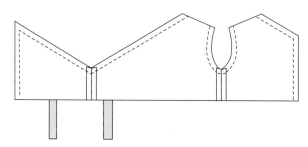

Figure 3

5. Sew shoulder seam; press.

6. Baste the bottom edges of bodice and lining together.

7. Sew short ends of 5 x 22-inch skirt together, ending 2½ inches from top. Press under ¼-inch on open section of the seam and topstitch (Figure 4).

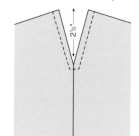

Figure 4

8. Press and sew a doubled ¼-inch hem along bottom edge.

9. Gather top of skirt to fit to bodice bottom edge. Sew in place; press seam toward skirt.

10. Lap left side of back bodice piece over the right side and sew a snap set at the top neck edge, just above the skirt seam and one in between.

11. Press a ¼-inch hem at top edge of the 8 x 22-inch skirt strip. Fold over an additional ½ inch and stitch close to edge to form a casing for elastic.

12. Thread elastic through casing. Pin ends of elastic even with edges of skirt and stitch to secure (Figure 5).

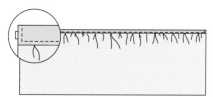

Figure 5

13. Sew short ends together for center back seam.

14. Press ¼-inch hem along skirt bottom. Fold up an additional ½ inch and stitch.

Purse

1. To make straps, sew one 1 x 6-inch green dot and floral print strip together along both long edges and across one short end. Trim corners and turn right side out; press. Topstitch ⅛ inch from edges. Repeat with second set of strips.

2. Place a finished strap, right sides together, on the green dot purse front and back as indicated on pattern. Baste in place (Figure 6).

Figure 6

3. Sew a green dot D purse section to a floral print D lining section along the top straight edges. Repeat with second set.

4. Pin the two pieced purse/lining sections together, matching purse sides and lining sides and having straps tucked up away from the seam line. Sew all around, leaving a 2-inch opening on one side of lining half (Figure 7). Clip curves and turn right side out through opening.

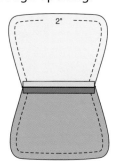

2"

Figure 7

5. Hand- or machine-stitch opening closed and tuck the lining into the purse; press.

6. To make the ruffles, sew short ends of each ruffle strip together. Press and sew a ¼-inch hem at bottom of each ruffle strip. Fold top edge of each strip under ⅜ inch and sew a row of gathering stitches ¼ inch from fold.

7. Pull gathering stitches on 10-inch-long strip to fit top edge of the purse. Carefully add fabric adhesive to wrong side of ruffle along the gathering row and press ruffle in place. Repeat with the 10½-inch strip and fit it to the purse right under first ruffle. Repeat with 11-inch strip, gathering it to fit under second strip.

8. Tie strap ends in a knot to finish the purse. *Note: By tying the straps near the ends, the purse becomes a shoulder bag. If you prefer a shorter purse to hang at the wrist, tie ends closer to purse.* ■

Casual Saturday

The bright pink wristlet adds the finishing touch to this Casual Saturday ensemble of bright pink jeans and white hoodie.

Hoodie, Wristlet & Jeans

Materials
- 5½ x 3¼-inch scrap pink print for wristlet lining
- ⅓ yard raspberry pink denim for jeans and wristlet
- ⅓ yard white sweatshirt fleece for hoodie
- Coordinating-color all-purpose thread
- 3-inch-wide white ribbing for hoodie
- 5 inches ⅜-inch-wide elastic
- 6-inch separating zipper
- 5¾ inches ¼-inch-wide pink grosgrain ribbon for wristlet handle
- 2 inches white elastic cord for wristlet closure
- ⅜–⅝-inch-diameter white shank button for wristlet closure
- Small white iron-on flower trim
- Basic sewing supplies and equipment

Cutting
Use pattern templates G, II, JJ, KK, LL, MM, NN and OO (pages 48, 58, 60–63) for Casual Saturday. Transfer pattern markings to fabric.

From raspberry pink denim:
- Cut two jeans fronts (II), reversing one.
- Cut two jeans backs (JJ), reversing one.
- Cut two pockets (G), reversing one.
- Cut one 1½ x 13½-inch strip for jeans waistband.
- Cut one 5½ x 3¼-inch rectangle for wristlet.

From white sweatshirt fleece:
- Cut one hoodie back (KK) on fold of fabric.
- Cut two hoodie fronts (LL), reversing one.
- Cut two hoods (MM), reversing one.
- Cut two sleeves (NN) on fold of fabric.
- Cut two hoodie pockets (OO), reversing one.

From white ribbing:
- Cut two 1¼ x 3½-inch strips for sleeve cuffs.
- Cut one 2½ x 12½-inch strip for bottom band.

Assembly

Stitch right sides together using a ¼-inch seam allowance, pressing seams open, unless otherwise directed.

Jeans

Note: Topstitching on jeans is sewn with a contrasting color of thread (in this model white was used) and a double line of stitching to look more like commercial jeans. A twin needle could be used for this doubled stitching.

1. Press a ¼-inch hem on the diagonal side of each pocket. Topstitch ⅛ inch from seam and again ⅛ inch away.

2. Press long side and bottom edge of each pocket ¼ inch to wrong side. Pin a pocket to each jeans front with right sides up and edges even with jeans front. Topstitch ⅛ inch from folded edge and again ⅛ inch away (Figure 1).

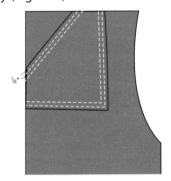

Figure 1

3. Sew center front seam. Press seam to one side and topstitch close to seam line and ⅛ inch away, sewing through all three layers (Figure 2).

Figure 2

4. Sew center back seam.

5. Sew front to back at one side. Press seam toward back and topstitch, through three layers, close to seam and ⅛ inch away. Repeat with other side seam.

6. Finish bottom edge of legs with a zigzag stitch or serged edges. Press a ½-inch hem to the wrong side and topstitch ⅜ inch and ¼ inch from bottom edge.

7. Finish one long edge of waistband strip with a zigzag stitch or serged edges.

8. Sew short ends of waistband together for center back.

9. Sew long unfinished edge of waistband to top of jeans (Figure 3).

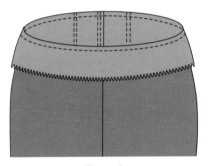

Figure 3

10. Fold waistband over to inside of jeans so waistband is ½ inch wide. Topstitch waistband close to seam, leaving 1 inch open at each side seam so elastic can be inserted into casing.

11. Thread elastic into back waistband casing and secure it at each side seam by stitching across ends (Figure 4). Sew opening closed.

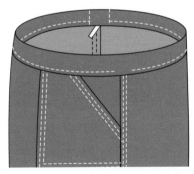

Figure 4

12. Topstitch top edge of waistband.

13. Sew inner leg seam to finish.

Hoodie Sweatshirt

1. Press and sew a ¼-inch hem on curved side of each pocket (Figure 5).

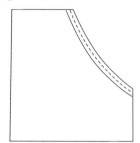

Figure 5

2. Fold top and short edges of pockets ¼ inch to wrong side and pin one pocket to each sweatshirt front with right sides up and raw edges even. Stitch across top and short side of each pocket (Figure 6). Baste long sides and bottom edge.

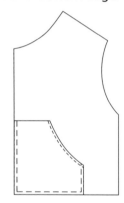

Figure 6

3. Sew fronts and back together at shoulder seams.

4. Sew hood halves together along curved back seam (Figure 7). With seam pressed open, topstitch ⅛ inch from seam on both sides.

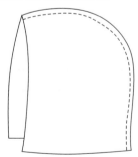

Figure 7

5. Finish front edge of hood with zigzag stitch or serged edge. Fold edge ¾ inch to wrong side and stitch.

6. Pin and sew hood to neck edge, matching edge of hood to dots on front neck and easing in hood as necessary. With seam folded toward sweatshirt (pin if necessary), topstitch close to seam (Figure 8).

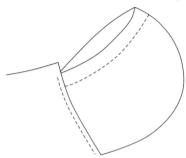

Figure 8

7. Fold each sleeve ribbing strip in half lengthwise with wrong sides facing. Sew a ribbing strip to the end of each sleeve, stretching ribbing to fit. If desired, use zigzag stitch or serging for this seam. With seam folded toward sleeve, topstitch close to seam (Figure 9).

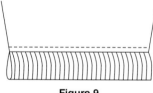

Figure 9

8. Gather top of sleeves between dots to fit armholes and sew sleeves to sweatshirt body. With seam folded toward sleeve, topstitch close to seam.

9. Stitch entire underarm seam (Figure 10).

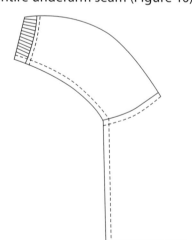

Figure 10

10. Fold bottom band ribbing in half lengthwise with wrong sides facing. Sew to bottom edge of sweatshirt, stretching ribbing to fit. If desired, use zigzag stitch or serging for this seam. With seam folded toward sweatshirt, topstitch close to seam.

11. Fold front edges of sweatshirt (including ribbing) ¼ inch to wrong side. Separate zipper halves and pin or baste left side of front to left side of zipper and sew in place. *Note: Check to be sure zipper head can still slide up and down before stitching.* Repeat with right front side and right side of zipper.

Wristlet

1. Fold the 5½ x 3¼ inch denim rectangle in half right sides together so it measures 2¾ x 3¼ inches and sew side seams (fold will be bottom of bag) (Figure 11). Repeat with lining. Turn bag right side out, leaving lining unturned.

Figure 11

2. Press a ¼-inch hem to the wrong side on denim and lining top edges.

3. Fold ribbon in half and insert ¼ inch into bag next to side seam; baste to secure. Fold elastic cord in half and insert ends ¼ inch into bag top at center back; baste to secure (Figure 12).

Figure 12

4. Insert lining into bag with folded top edges even and matching side seams. Topstitch all around top edge.

5. Sew button to center front.

6. Follow manufacturer's directions to iron flower trim to front bottom corner. ■

Puppy Love

Every little girl needs a puppy. Stitch up the perfect pet and accessories for your doll.

Puppy, Collar & Bed
Materials
- Fat quarter green tonal for collar and leash
- 2 coordinating flannel fat quarters for bed
- ¼ yard brown velour
- Coordinating-color and black all-purpose thread
- 3 (¼-inch-diameter) black buttons for puppy's eyes and nose
- 5 (¼-inch-diameter) iron-on silver studs for collar
- Snap set for collar
- Small charm for puppy tag
- 7mm jump ring for collar
- Lanyard hook for leash
- Scrap of thin batting or fleece
- Fiberfill
- Basic sewing supplies and equipment

Cutting
Use pattern templates PP, QQ, RR and SS (pages 59, 61, 63) for Puppy Love. Transfer pattern markings to fabric.

From green tonal:
- Cut two 1 x 5½-inch strips for collar.
- Cut one 1½ x 12½-inch strip for leash.

From coordinating flannel fat quarters:
- Cut two 6½ x 5½-inch rectangles from one flannel for bed.
- Cut two 2½ x 20½-inch strips from coordinating flannel for ruffle trim.

From brown velour:
- Cut two puppy bodies (SS), reversing one.
- Cut four ears (QQ).
- Cut one head insert (RR).
- Cut two puppy body under sections (PP), reversing one.

Assembly

Stitch right sides together using a ¼-inch seam allowance, pressing seams open, unless otherwise directed.

Puppy

1. To make each ear, sew two ear pieces together, leaving top open (Figure 1). Clip curves and turn right side out.

Figure 1

2. Fold a small pleat at top of each ear; baste to hold through all layers (Figure 2).

Figure 2

3. Pin an ear to the right side of each body section as marked on pattern for positioning. Baste in place.

4. Stitch body pieces together along back, tail and down to dot under tail. Stitch from nose to dot under head (Figure 3). Clip curves.

Figure 3

5. To add head insert, pin the insert in place, matching dots at nose end and back of head. Pin long sides of insert to sides of head. Stitch each side, stopping at each end to backstitch and cut the thread (Figure 4). Reposition needle on other side of dot and sew to next dot.

Figure 4

6. Join two body under sections at straight edge, leaving open where marked on pattern (Figure 5).

Figure 5

7. Pin and stitch the under section to the upper body, matching seams and dots. Clip curves and turn right side out through opening.

8. Stuff body firmly with fiberfill. Fold opening seam allowance to the inside and slipstitch opening closed.

9. Using doubled black thread, sew a black button to the head for an eye. Insert needle into head to come out at the other eye position and add second button. Pull thread to form a slight indentation; knot and clip thread. Sew third button to snout for nose.

Collar & Leash

1. To make collar, place the two 1 x 5½-inch fabric strips right sides together and pin to batting scrap. Sew all around, leaving a 2-inch opening along one side. Trim corners and turn right side out. Press. Turn opening seam to the inside; press.

2. Topstitch all around, ⅛ inch from edge.

3. Follow manufacturer's directions to iron silver studs to one side of collar, starting in center and spacing them ½ inch apart.

4. Overlap one end over the other and sew a snap set.

5. Sew charm to edge of collar below snap closure.

6. Sew jump ring to edge of collar at center back so leash can attach to collar (Figure 6).

Figure 6

7. To make leash, fold strip in half lengthwise and stitch raw edges, leaving a 3-inch opening on one side (Figure 7). Trim corners and turn right side out.

Figure 7

8. Fold in seam allowance of the opening and press strip. Topstitch all around.

9. Fold one end over 2 inches and stitch end down securely to make loop for hand—first check to be sure loop will fit doll's hand.

10. Sew lanyard to other end of leash.

11. Attach lanyard to jump ring on collar.

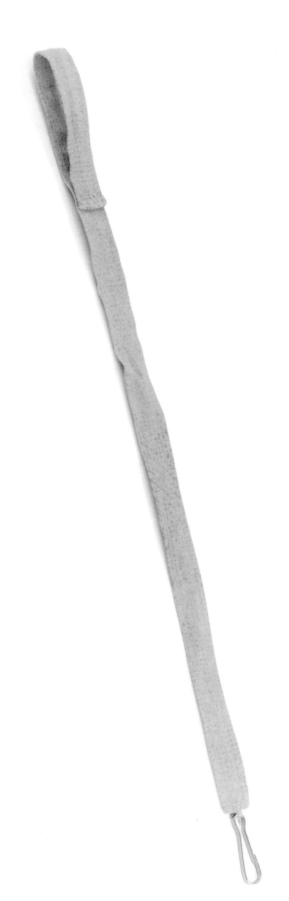

Puppy Bed

1. Sew the two ruffle strips together along short ends to form a circle (Figure 8).

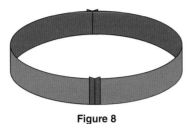

Figure 8

2. Fold and press ruffle strip in half lengthwise, wrong sides together.

3. Sew two rows of gathering stitches along raw edge, ¼ inch and ⅛ inch from edge.

4. Fold ruffle to divide it into four equal sections and mark with pins. Mark the center of each side of one of the bed rectangles with pins. Pull bobbin threads to gather ruffle to fit the rectangle, right sides facing and matching the quarter-mark pins. Distribute gathers evenly and sew in place (Figure 9).

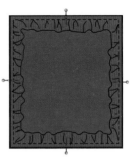

Figure 9

5. Place remaining bed rectangle over the ruffled piece and sew all around, leaving a 3-inch opening along one side. Trim corners and turn right side out.

6. Stuff the bed loosely with fiberfill. Fold in seam allowances of the opening and slipstitch opening closed to finish. ■

Classy Coat

Let the snow fly! This stylish coat, beret and boots will keep your doll warm throughout the winter.

Coat, Beret & Boots

Materials
- ⅛ yard magenta faux suede
- ⅛ yard black pleather (faux leather with knit backing)
- ½ yard gray faux suede
- 1¼ x 7-inch scrap gray fur or plush felt
- Coordinating-color all-purpose thread
- 3 small snap sets
- 6 (⁷⁄₁₆-inch-diameter) black shank buttons
- 5 inches ½-inch-wide black hook-and-loop tape
- Permanent fabric adhesive (optional)
- Basic sewing supplies and equipment

Cutting
Use pattern templates S, T, U, V, W, X, Y, Z, AA, BB and CC for Classy Coat (pages 52–55 and 59). Transfer pattern markings to fabric.

From magenta faux suede:
- Cut two 1¼ x 13½-inch strips for hatband.
- Cut 12 flower petals (U) as directed in the Assembly instructions.

From black pleather:
- Cut two boot soles (AA), reversing one.
- Cut two boot legs (BB), reversing one.
- Cut two boot uppers (CC), reversing one.

From gray faux suede:
- Cut two pockets (S).
- Cut two sleeves (T), reversing one.
- Cut two front facings (V), reversing one.
- Cut two collars (W) on fold of fabric, reversing one.
- Cut one bodice back (X) on fold of fabric.
- Cut two bodice fronts (Y), reversing one.
- Cut one back facing (Z) on fold of fabric.
- Cut one 7½ x 22-inch strip for coat skirt.
- Cut one 7-inch-diameter circle for beret.

From gray fur or plush felt:
- Cut two ⅝ x 7-inch strips for boot tops.

Assembly

Stitch right sides together using a ¼-inch seam allowance, pressing seams open, unless otherwise directed.

Coat

1. Sew bodice fronts to back at shoulder seams.

2. Turn under and stitch the lower edge of each sleeve ¾ inch to hem.

3. Sew a row of gathering stitches to top of each sleeve between the dots (Figure 1). Gather each sleeve to fit the armhole, matching dots and shoulder seam. Sew armhole seam; press seam toward sleeve.

Figure 1

4. Sew entire underarm seam and side seam (Figure 2).

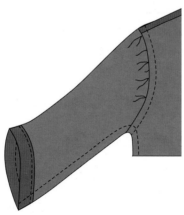

Figure 2

5. To make the pocket, sew the two pocket pieces together, leaving open at top. Clip curves and turn right side out.

6. Fold in seam allowance at top edge and topstitch across ⅛ inch from fold.

7. Pin pocket to coat skirt 2¾ inches from bottom edge and 2½ inches in from right edge. Topstitch pocket in place (Figure 3).

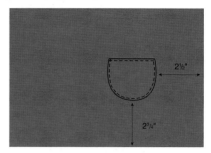

Figure 3

8. Gather top edge of coat skirt, starting and ending ¾ inch from each end. Insert a pin 6 inches from each end for a placement mark. Pull up gathers to fit coat bodice, matching the pins to side seams. Sew together; press seam toward coat bodice.

9. On outside, topstitch close to seam on the bodice side (Figure 4).

Figure 4

10. Sew the two collar pieces together, leaving neck edge open. Clip curves and turn right side out; press (Figure 5). Topstitch close to seam.

Figure 5

11. Pin collar to neck edge of coat bodice, with collar and coat right side up. Match center backs, dots on collar to shoulder seams and ends of collar to dots on bodice front. Machine-baste in place ³⁄₁₆ inch from edge.

12. Sew V front facing to Z back facing at shoulder seams; press.

13. Pin facing to coat fronts and neck edge (over collar) matching shoulder seams. Sew facing in place starting and stopping ¾ inch up from front bottom edge (Figure 6). Clip curves and trim corners.

Figure 6

14. Trim facing ½ inch from bottom edge again referring to figure 6. Stitch through facing and bottom edge of coat ¼ inch from trimmed edge.

15. Turn facing to inside of coat and press, folding up ¾ inch along bottom edge of coat for hem; sew in place (Figure 7). Tack facing to shoulder seam allowances.

Figure 7

16. On outside, lift collar and topstitch coat back close to neck seam, stitching between shoulder seams (Figure 8).

Figure 8

17. Overlap right coat front over left to end of collar. Sew two snap sets to top edge and one just above skirt seam (Figure 9).

Figure 9

18. Sew four buttons to right side of coat, referring to photo for placement.

19. To make flower embellishment for the pocket and beret, trace petal pattern (U) 12 times on the wrong side of the remaining magenta faux suede, leaving a generous ¼ inch between shapes. Fold fabric in half with right sides facing and traced petals on top. Stitch directly on pattern lines, leaving open at bottom (Figure 10). Cut out each petal ⅛ inch from seam. Clip curves and turn right side out.

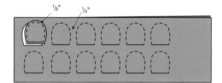

Figure 10

20. Thread a needle with doubled matching thread and hand-stitch a few gathering stitches ⅛ inch from the bottom of a petal. Pick up a second petal and continue gathering (Figure 11). Repeat until there are 6 petals on the thread.

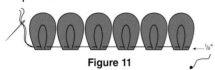

Figure 11

21. Take a stitch into the first petal to form a circle. Pull on thread to gather petals into a tight circle (Figure 12). Knot thread but do not clip. Push shank of button into flower center and attach with a few stitches.

Figure 12

22. Repeat steps 20 and 21 for second flower.

23. Tack or glue one flower to coat pocket, near top. Set aside second flower for beret.

Beret

1. Sew the two 1¼ x 13½-inch strips magenta faux suede together along one long edge.

2. Join the short ends to form a circle for hatband.

3. Sew gathering stitches ¼ inch from outside edge of the hat circle. Pull gathers to fit edge of circle with one long edge of the hatband; sew in place (Figure 13).

Figure 13

4. Press a ¼-inch hem to wrong side on the other long edge of hatband. Fold hatband at seam line and pin folded edge over hat/hatband seam. Topstitch both edges of hatband, catching inside band edge in the stitches.

5. Tack or glue remaining flower to hatband front, about 1½ inches from center (Figure 14).

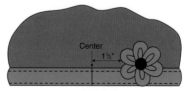

Figure 14

Boots

1. Fold and sew a ¼-inch hem at top edge of each boot-leg section (Figure 15).

← ¼"

Figure 15

2. Pin inner (concave) side of each boot upper to the lower edge of the matching boot-leg section. Clip curves (Figure 16).

Figure 16

3. Cut hook-and-loop tape into two 2½-inch lengths and separate hook and loop sides. Referring to pattern for placement, sew a hook strip on the right side of boot leg, from boot top to seam. Sew loop strip on wrong side of other edge, from boot top to seam (Figure 17). **Note:** *The hook side will overlap loop side to close boot.* Repeat with second boot and hook-and-loop strip.

Figure 17

4. Overlap boot ends and close hook-and-loop tape. Take a few stitches at lower edge of boot upper pieces to hold ends together.

5. Pin a matching sole to each upper boot section, matching dots; stitch. Clip curves and turn right side out.

6. Glue a ⅝ x 7-inch strip of fur trim to the top of each boot, starting at the edge of hook side of the hook-and-loop tape. Trim excess fur so ends just meet when boot is closed (Figure 18). ■

Figure 18

Back to School

Your doll is ready to head back to school in this ensemble of denim skirt, leggings and top. The fashionable tote is just right for carrying all the essentials.

Top, Leggings, Skirt & Tote

Materials

- ¼ yard "acid" denim for skirt and tote
- ½ yard red knit fabric for top and leggings
- Scrap of red-and-blue print for tote lining
- Coordinating-color all-purpose thread
- Size 8 red pearl cotton or red embroidery floss
- 4 small snap sets
- 22 inches ⅜-inch-wide elastic
- 15 (¼-inch-diameter) iron-on silver studs
- 15 inches ¼-inch-diameter red cord for tote handle
- Embroidery needle
- Permanent fabric adhesive
- Basic sewing supplies and equipment

Cutting

Use pattern templates for J, K, L, M, N and O (pages 50–53) Back to School. Transfer pattern markings to fabric.

From denim:
- Cut one 7¼ x 15-inch rectangle for skirt.
- Cut two 3½ x 3½-inch squares for tote.

From red knit:
- Cut two leggings fronts (J), reversing one.
- Cut two leggings backs (L), reversing one.
- Cut one top front (K) following cutting line for school top.
- Cut two top backs (M), reversing one, and following cutting line for Back to School.
- Cut one neck facing (N) on fold of fabric.
- Cut two sleeves (O), reversing one.

From red-and-blue print:
- Cut two 3½-inch squares for tote lining.

From the elastic:
- Cut two 11-inch lengths.

Assembly

Stitch right sides together using a ¼-inch seam allowance, pressing seams open, unless otherwise directed.

Leggings

1. Sew fronts to backs at side seams.

2. Sew center front seam (Figure 1).

Figure 1

3. To form casing, fold a ⅝-inch hem to wrong side at top of leggings. Stitch close to the raw edge (Figure 2).

Figure 2

4. Thread one elastic length into casing. Pin ends of elastic even with edges of leggings and stitch to secure (Figure 3).

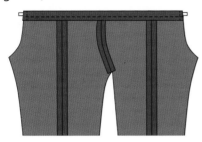

Figure 3

5. Press a ½-inch hem to the wrong side at the lower edge of each leg; stitch.

6. Sew center back seam.

7. Sew inner leg seam, matching center front and back seams (Figure 4).

Figure 4

Top

1. Sew front to the two back sections at shoulder seams.

2. Fold a ¾-inch hem to inside on each sleeve; stitch in place.

3. With right sides together, pin sleeve to armhole of top body, matching dots and arrow on the sleeve with shoulder seam. Stitch and press seam toward sleeve. Repeat with second sleeve.

4. Sew front and back together at underarm seams from hemmed edge of sleeve to bottom edge of top (Figure 5).

Figure 5

5. Sew ends of neck facing to short ends of facing extension on top back. Pin facing to neck edge, matching shoulder seams. Sew neck-edge seam (Figure 6). Clip curves and trim corners.

Figure 6

6. With facing extensions still folded to right side, stitch facing to back of top, ¾ inch up from bottom edge (Figure 7).

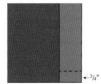

Figure 7

7. Trim and remove the bottom section of facing close to the stitching (Figure 8).

Figure 8

8. Turn facing to inside. Press seam and press up a ¾-inch bottom hem. Stitch hem (Figure 9).

Figure 9

9. Sew facing in place by sewing ½ inch all around front and neck edges.

10. Overlap right back edge over left. Sew four snap sets evenly spaced down opening (Figure 10).

Figure 10

11. Follow manufacturer's directions to iron five silver studs along front neck edge. ***Note:*** *Refer to photo for positioning.*

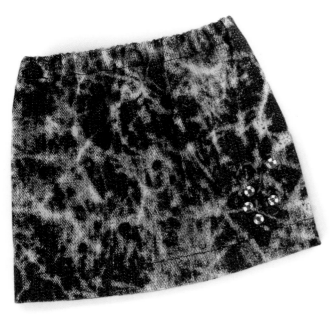

Tote

1. Transfer embroidery motif given on page 51 about ⅝ inch from side and bottom edge on the left side of one 3½-inch denim square. ***Note:*** *The motif is flipped upside down from the skirt placement.*

2. Sew a running stitch on the marked lines using 1 strand of red pearl cotton or 3 strands of embroidery floss. (Do not apply the studs at this time.)

3. With right sides facing, stitch the two denim squares along sides and bottom edge. Trim corners and turn right side out.

4. Repeat step 3 with lining squares, but do not turn right side out.

5. Press a ¼-inch hem at the top of denim and lining pieces.

6. Insert lining into denim bag. With the folded top edges even, topstitch all around top edge, catching lining in the stitches.

7. Follow manufacturer's directions to iron five silver studs to the embroidered motif.

8. Tie a knot on each end of the red cord and using the permanent fabric adhesive, carefully glue a knotted end to each side of tote top for a cross-body strap. ■

Skirt

1. Sew the two short ends of the 7¼ x 15-inch denim rectangle together for center back seam.

2. Serge or zigzag-stitch bottom long edge to finish edge. Fold a ¾-inch hem to wrong side and stitch.

3. Press a ¼-inch hem at top edge. Fold down an additional ⅝ inch and press to make casing. Stitch close to edge, leaving 1 inch open at center back.

4. Thread elastic into casing through opening in back. Overlap ends of elastic and stitch to secure (Figure 11).

Figure 11

5. Sew opening in casing closed.

6. Transfer embroidery motif given on page 51 to right side of skirt front, about 1 inch up from bottom edge and a little off to one side. Sew a running stitch on the pattern lines using 1 strand of red pearl cotton or 3 strands of embroidery floss.

7. Follow the manufacturer's directions to iron five silver studs to the design where indicated on the pattern.

Holiday Flair

Polka dots decorate this fun holiday set. Wear the dress with or without the jacket for different occasions. A headband and necklace complete the look.

Dress, Jacket, Headband & Necklace

Materials
- 1 fat eighth white solid for bodice lining
- 1 fat quarter white-with-black dots for bodice
- 1 fat quarter black-with-white dots for skirt and jacket lining
- 1 fat quarter red-with-black dots for jacket
- Scrap thin batting or fleece for headband
- Coordinating-color all-purpose thread
- 8 (⅝-inch-diameter) red ribbon roses
- 3 inches ½-inch-wide elastic
- 6 inches ⅛-inch-wide black satin ribbon
- 3 small snap sets
- 9-inch length of silver chain
- Small silver charm
- 3–5mm silver jump rings
- Small silver clasp set
- Chain-nose pliers
- Permanent fabric adhesive (optional)
- Basic sewing supplies and equipment

Cutting
Use pattern templates DD, EE, FF, GG and HH (pages 56–58) for Holiday Flair. Transfer pattern markings to fabric.

From white solid:
- Cut two bodice backs (DD), reversing one, for lining.
- Cut one bodice front (EE) on fold of fabric for lining.

From white-with-black dots:
- Cut two bodice backs (DD), reversing one.
- Cut one bodice front (EE) on fold of fabric.
- Cut two 1⅛ x 10-inch strips for headband.

From black-with-white dots:
- Cut one 7 x 14-inch strip for skirt front.
- Cut two 7 x 7½-inch strips for skirt back.
- Cut one jacket back (FF) on fold of fabric for jacket lining
- Cut two jacket fronts (GG), reversing one, for jacket lining.

From red-with-black dots:
- Cut one jacket back (FF) on fold of fabric.
- Cut two jacket fronts (GG), reversing one.
- Cut two jacket sleeves (HH).

From batting scrap:
- Cut one 1⅛ x 10-inch strip for headband.

Assembly
Stitch right sides together using a ¼-inch seam allowance, pressing seams open, unless otherwise directed.

Dress
1. Sew bodice front to bodice backs at shoulder seams. Repeat with lining front and backs.

2. Pin bodice and lining right sides together, matching shoulder seams. Sew center-back seams and around neck edge and each armhole (Figure 1). Clip curves and turn right side out; press.

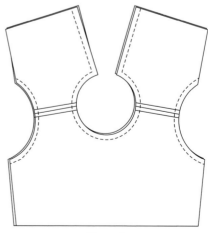

Figure 1

3. Pin lining front to lining back and bodice front to bodice back right sides together with raw edges even and matching armhole seams. Stitch together to complete side seams. Press seam flat wrong sides together.

4. Baste bodice and lining layers wrong sides together at open bottom edge.

5. Sew the two 7 x 7½-inch skirt backs together along one 7-inch side, ending 2½ inches from the top. Press ¼-inch under along open seam edges and topstitch (Figure 2).

Figure 2

6. Sew skirt back to skirt front at side seams.

7. Press a ¼-inch hem at bottom skirt edge. Fold up an additional ½ inch; pin and stitch to finish bottom-edge hem.

8. Gather top long raw edge of skirt to fit bottom edge of bodice, matching side seams and center back. Sew seam and press toward skirt.

9. Overlap the right side of bodice back over left and sew three snap sets spaced evenly down bodice back.

10. Tack or carefully glue five ribbon roses to dress front at waistline.

Jacket

1. Sew jacket fronts to jacket back at shoulder seams. Repeat with lining fronts and back.

2. Pin jacket and lining right sides together, matching shoulder seams. Sew neck seam, front edges and bottom back (Figure 3). Clip curves and turn right side out. Press.

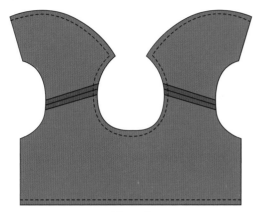

Figure 3

3. Press and sew a doubled ¼-inch hem on bottom edge of each sleeve.

4. Sew a row of gathering stitches between dots on each sleeve top. Gather sleeves to fit armhole, matching dots. Stitch seams and press toward sleeves.

5. Sew underarm seam.

6. If desired, flip front top corners of the jacket out to reveal contrast lining and tack in place.

Headband

1. Place the two 1⅛ x 10-inch fabric strips right sides together and pin to the same-size batting strip. Sew all around, leaving a 2-inch opening along one long side. Trim batting close to seam, trim corners and turn right side out; press.

2. Topstitch all around band.

3. Place ends of elastic ½ inch under ends of band; stitch securely (Figure 4).

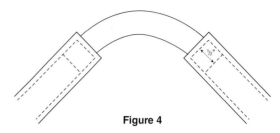

Figure 4

4. Glue three ribbon roses to the right side of band, with the middle rose about 1¼ inches from the center of the band.

5. Tie the black satin ribbon in a bow and glue just under bottom rose.

Necklace

1. Use jump ring to attach charm to chain. Open jump ring with chain nose pliers by twisting away from each other (not by pulling) (Figure 5). Slip ring end through hole in charm and use pliers to close the jump ring. Thread jump ring onto the chain.

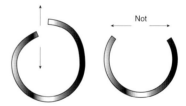

Figure 5

2. Open remaining two jump rings in the same manner and use them to attach ends of the clasp pieces, inserting one end of jump ring into end link of chain and then into hole in clasp to finish (Figure 6). ■

Figure 6

Patterns

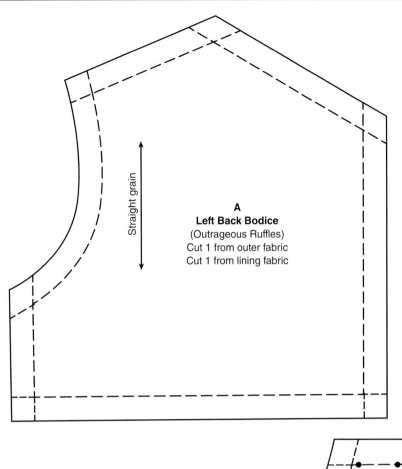

A
Left Back Bodice
(Outrageous Ruffles)
Cut 1 from outer fabric
Cut 1 from lining fabric

Straight grain

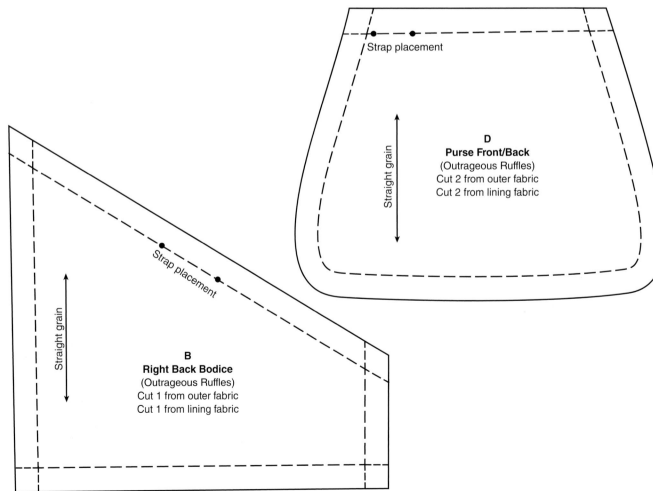

Strap placement

D
Purse Front/Back
(Outrageous Ruffles)
Cut 2 from outer fabric
Cut 2 from lining fabric

Straight grain

Straight grain

Strap placement

B
Right Back Bodice
(Outrageous Ruffles)
Cut 1 from outer fabric
Cut 1 from lining fabric

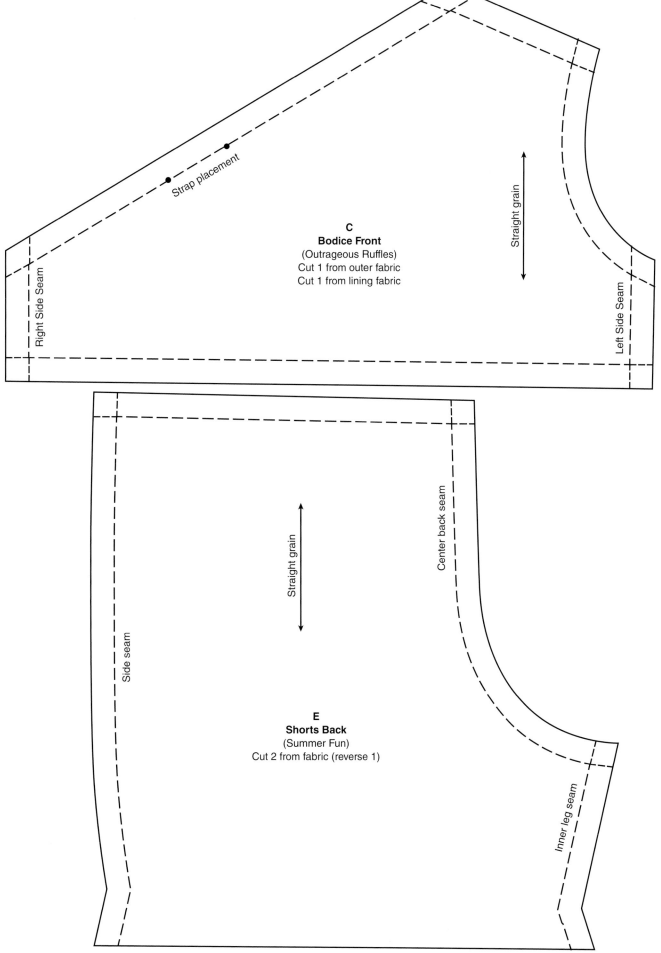

C
Bodice Front
(Outrageous Ruffles)
Cut 1 from outer fabric
Cut 1 from lining fabric

Strap placement

Straight grain

Right Side Seam

Left Side Seam

E
Shorts Back
(Summer Fun)
Cut 2 from fabric (reverse 1)

Straight grain

Center back seam

Side seam

Inner leg seam

Sew Trendy Fashions & Accessories for 18" Dolls

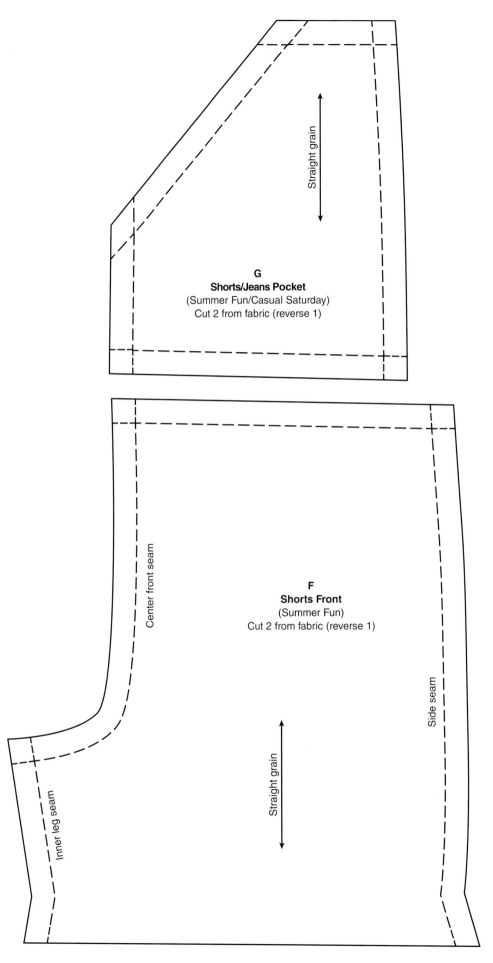

G
Shorts/Jeans Pocket
(Summer Fun/Casual Saturday)
Cut 2 from fabric (reverse 1)

Straight grain

F
Shorts Front
(Summer Fun)
Cut 2 from fabric (reverse 1)

Center front seam

Side seam

Inner leg seam

Straight grain

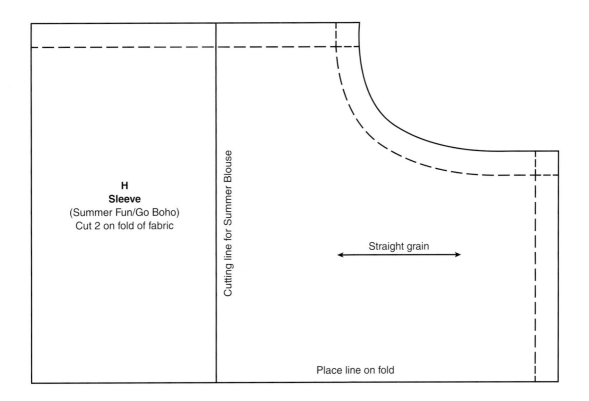

H
Sleeve
(Summer Fun/Go Boho)
Cut 2 on fold of fabric

Cutting line for Summer Blouse

Straight grain

Place line on fold

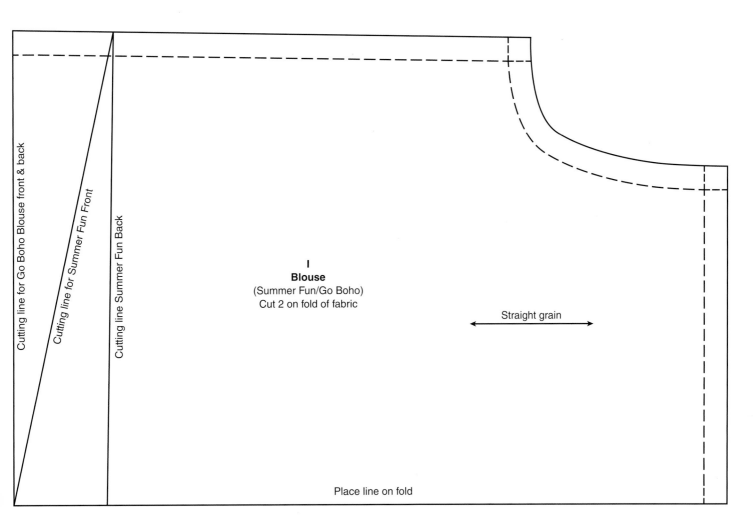

Cutting line for Go Boho Blouse front & back

Cutting line for Summer Fun Front

Cutting line Summer Fun Back

I
Blouse
(Summer Fun/Go Boho)
Cut 2 on fold of fabric

Straight grain

Place line on fold

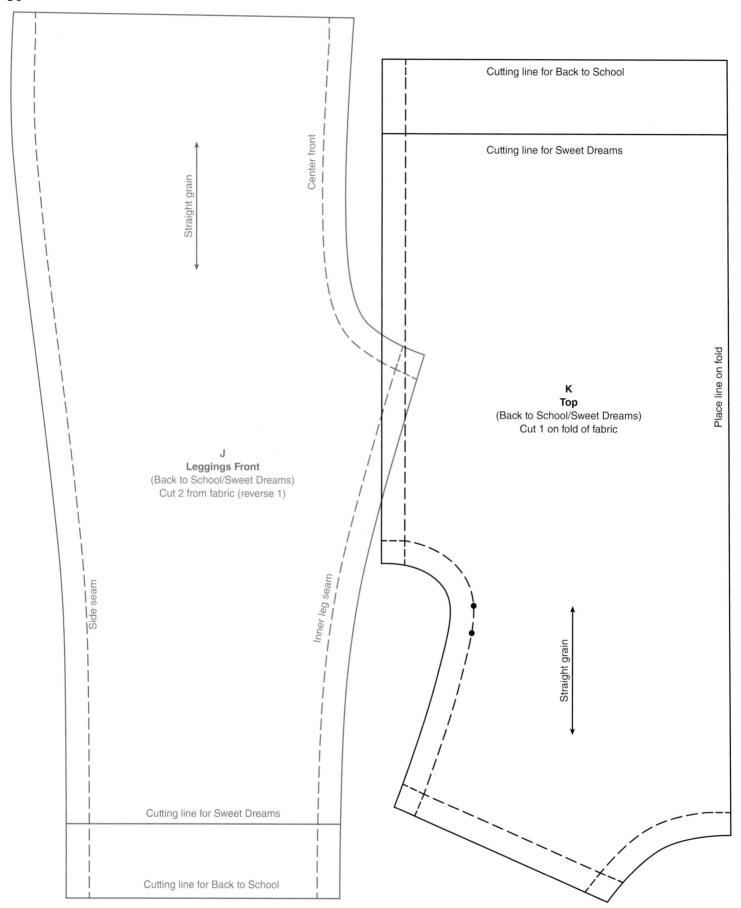

Straight grain

Center front

J
Leggings Front
(Back to School/Sweet Dreams)
Cut 2 from fabric (reverse 1)

Side seam

Inner leg seam

Cutting line for Sweet Dreams

Cutting line for Back to School

Cutting line for Back to School

Cutting line for Sweet Dreams

Place line on fold

K
Top
(Back to School/Sweet Dreams)
Cut 1 on fold of fabric

Straight grain

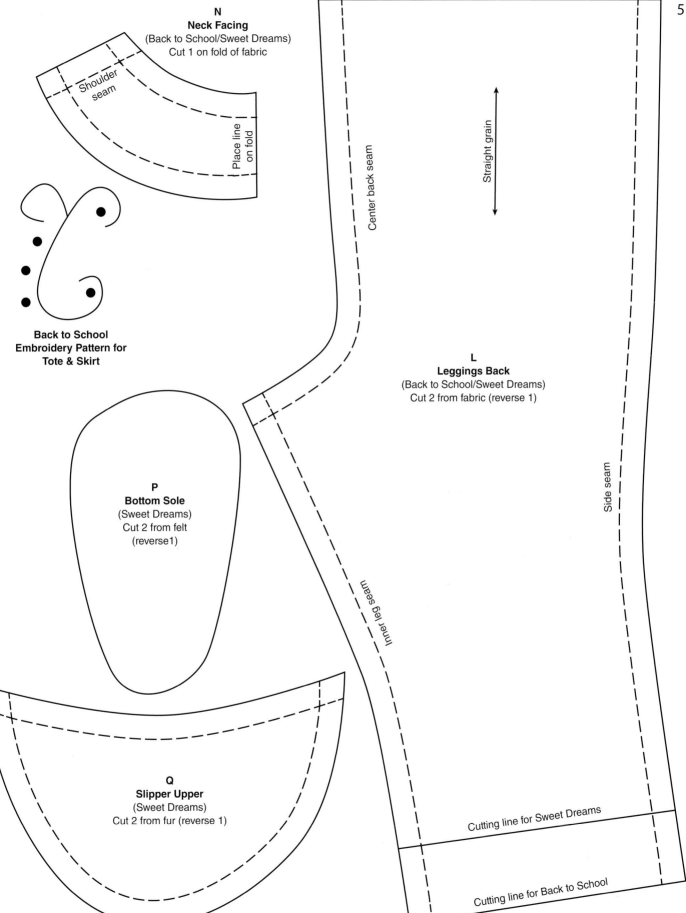

N
Neck Facing
(Back to School/Sweet Dreams)
Cut 1 on fold of fabric

Shoulder seam

Place line on fold

**Back to School
Embroidery Pattern for
Tote & Skirt**

P
Bottom Sole
(Sweet Dreams)
Cut 2 from felt
(reverse1)

Q
Slipper Upper
(Sweet Dreams)
Cut 2 from fur (reverse 1)

Center back seam

Straight grain

L
Leggings Back
(Back to School/Sweet Dreams)
Cut 2 from fabric (reverse 1)

Side seam

Inner leg seam

Cutting line for Sweet Dreams

Cutting line for Back to School

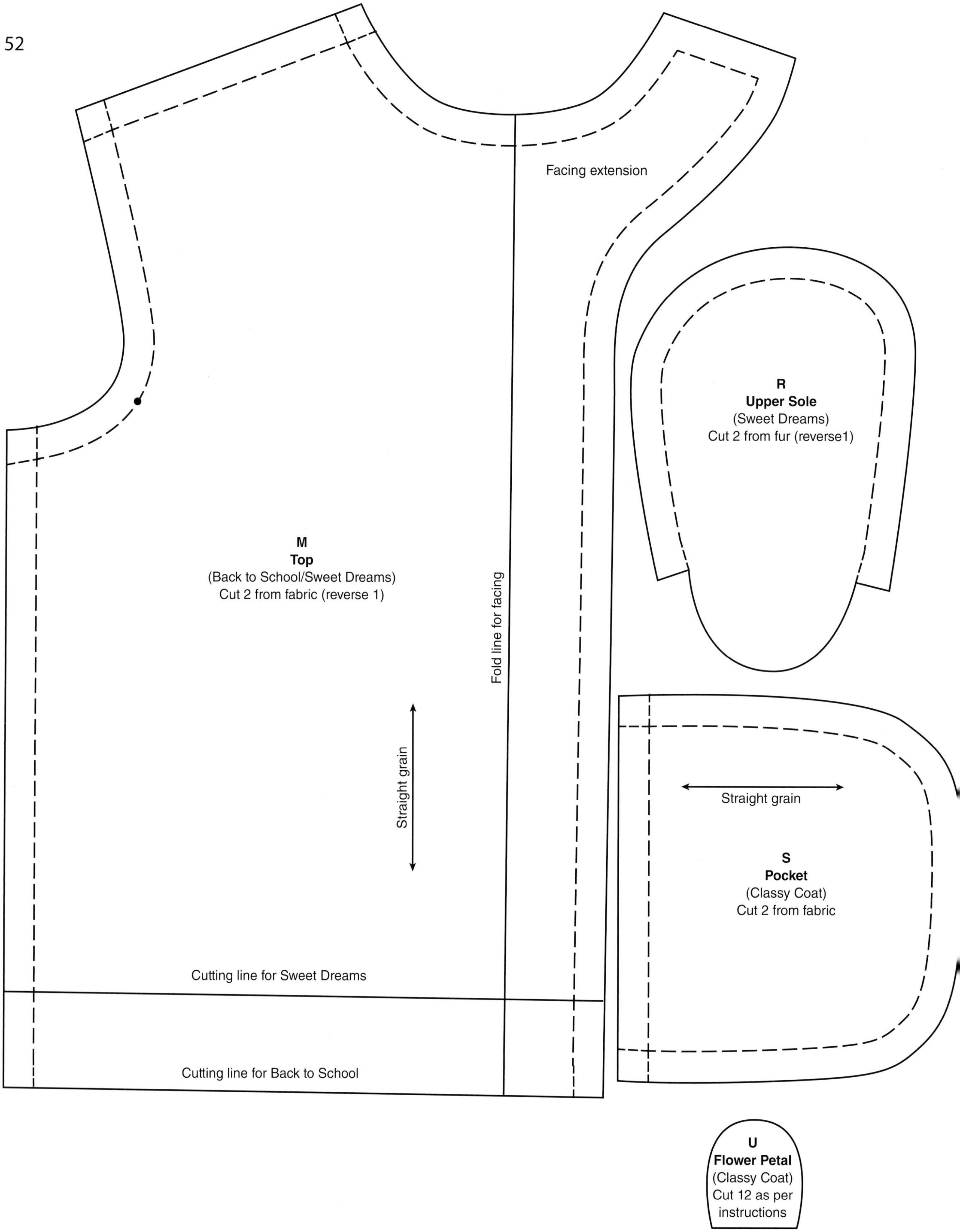

Facing extension

M
Top
(Back to School/Sweet Dreams)
Cut 2 from fabric (reverse 1)

Fold line for facing

Straight grain

Cutting line for Sweet Dreams

Cutting line for Back to School

R
Upper Sole
(Sweet Dreams)
Cut 2 from fur (reverse1)

Straight grain

S
Pocket
(Classy Coat)
Cut 2 from fabric

U
Flower Petal
(Classy Coat)
Cut 12 as per
instructions

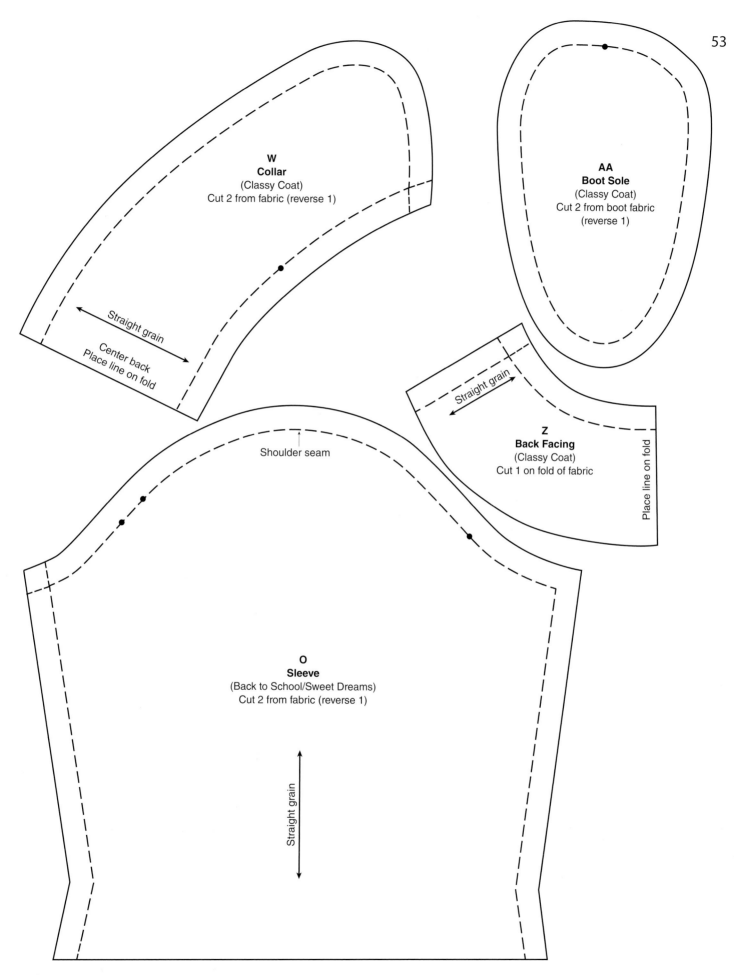

W
Collar
(Classy Coat)
Cut 2 from fabric (reverse 1)

Straight grain

Center back
Place line on fold

AA
Boot Sole
(Classy Coat)
Cut 2 from boot fabric
(reverse 1)

Straight grain

Z
Back Facing
(Classy Coat)
Cut 1 on fold of fabric

Place line on fold

Shoulder seam

O
Sleeve
(Back to School/Sweet Dreams)
Cut 2 from fabric (reverse 1)

Straight grain

Sew Trendy Fashions & Accessories for 18" Dolls

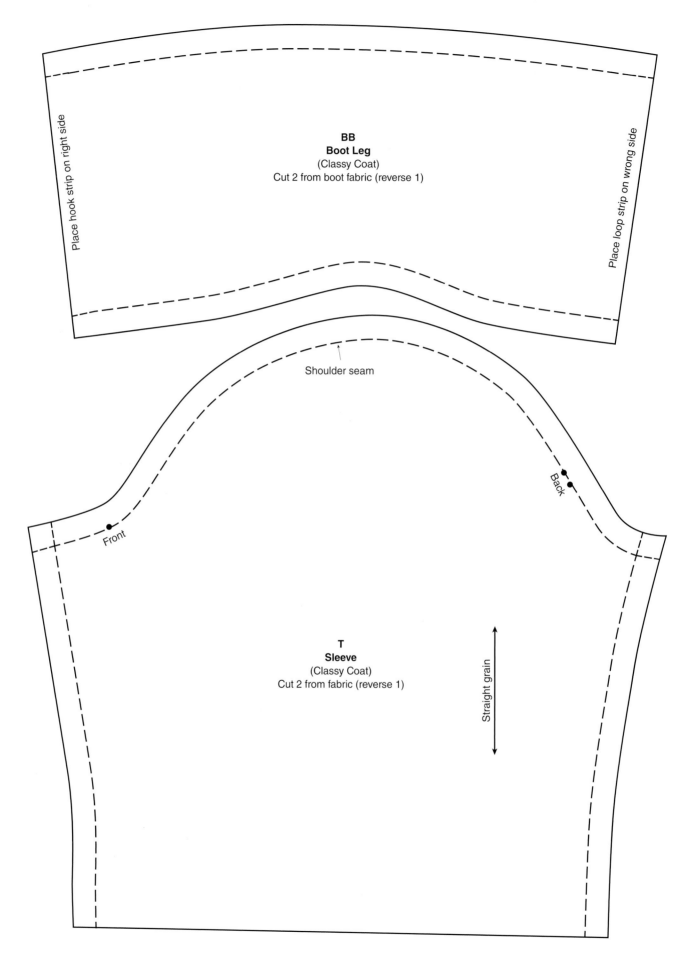

BB
Boot Leg
(Classy Coat)
Cut 2 from boot fabric (reverse 1)

Place hook strip on right side

Place loop strip on wrong side

Shoulder seam

Back

Front

T
Sleeve
(Classy Coat)
Cut 2 from fabric (reverse 1)

Straight grain

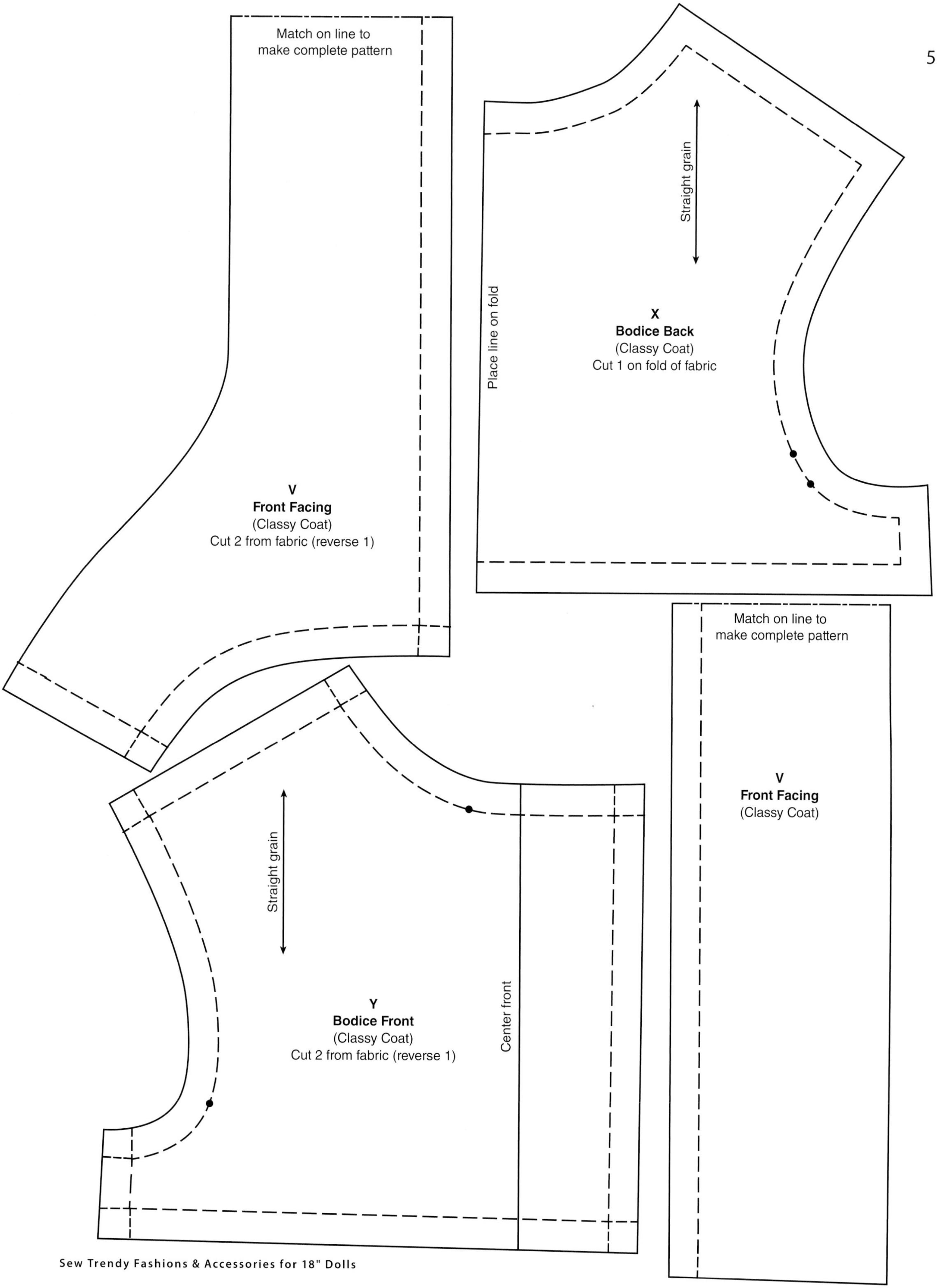

Match on line to
make complete pattern

55

V
Front Facing
(Classy Coat)
Cut 2 from fabric (reverse 1)

Straight grain

Place line on fold

X
Bodice Back
(Classy Coat)
Cut 1 on fold of fabric

Match on line to
make complete pattern

V
Front Facing
(Classy Coat)

Straight grain

Y
Bodice Front
(Classy Coat)
Cut 2 from fabric (reverse 1)

Center front

DD
Bodice Back
(Holiday Flair)
Cut 2 from outer fabric (reverse 1)
Cut 2 from lining fabric (reverse 1)

Straight grain

EE
Bodice Front
(Holiday Flair)
Cut 1 from outer fabric on fold
Cut 1 from lining fabric on fold

Straight grain

Place line on fold

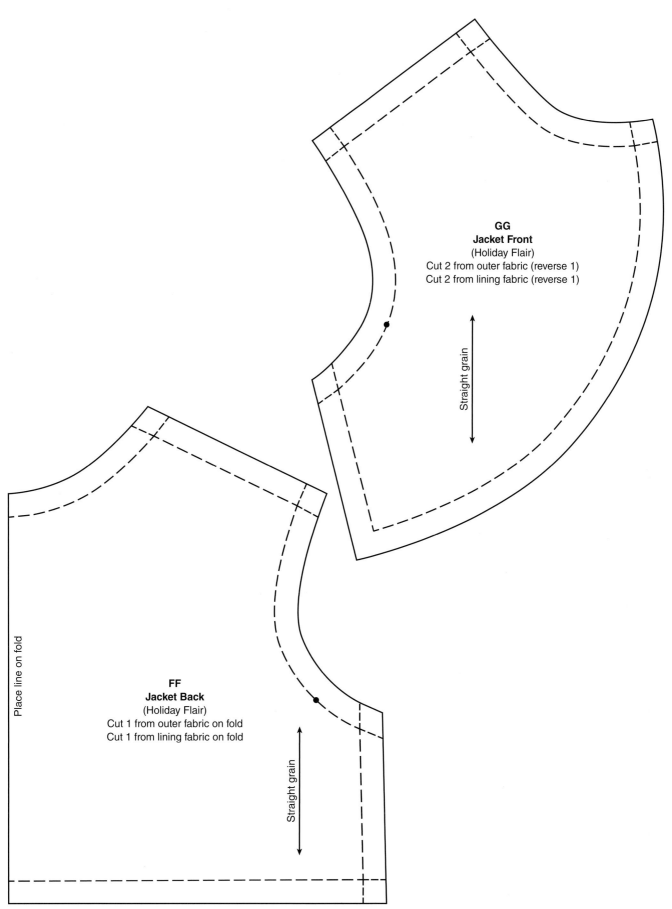

GG
Jacket Front
(Holiday Flair)
Cut 2 from outer fabric (reverse 1)
Cut 2 from lining fabric (reverse 1)

Straight grain

Place line on fold

FF
Jacket Back
(Holiday Flair)
Cut 1 from outer fabric on fold
Cut 1 from lining fabric on fold

Straight grain

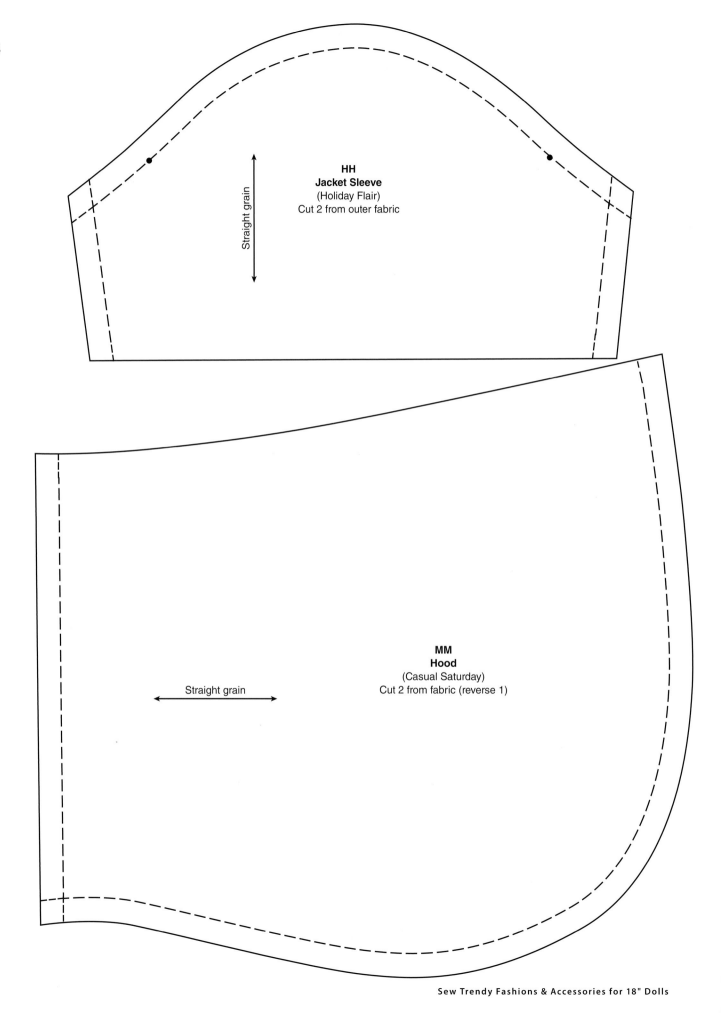

HH
Jacket Sleeve
(Holiday Flair)
Cut 2 from outer fabric

Straight grain

MM
Hood
(Casual Saturday)
Cut 2 from fabric (reverse 1)

Straight grain

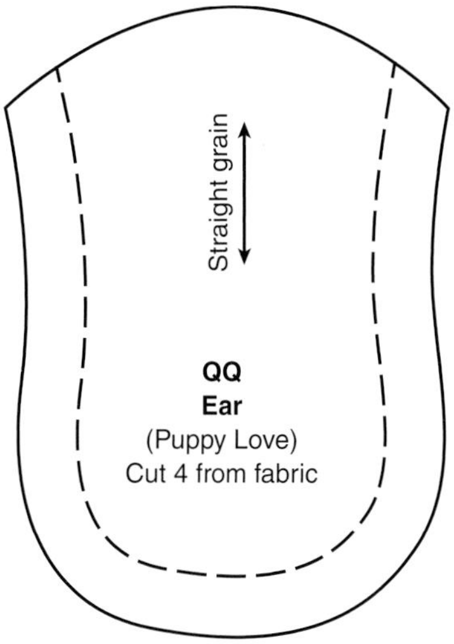

Straight grain

QQ
Ear
(Puppy Love)
Cut 4 from fabric

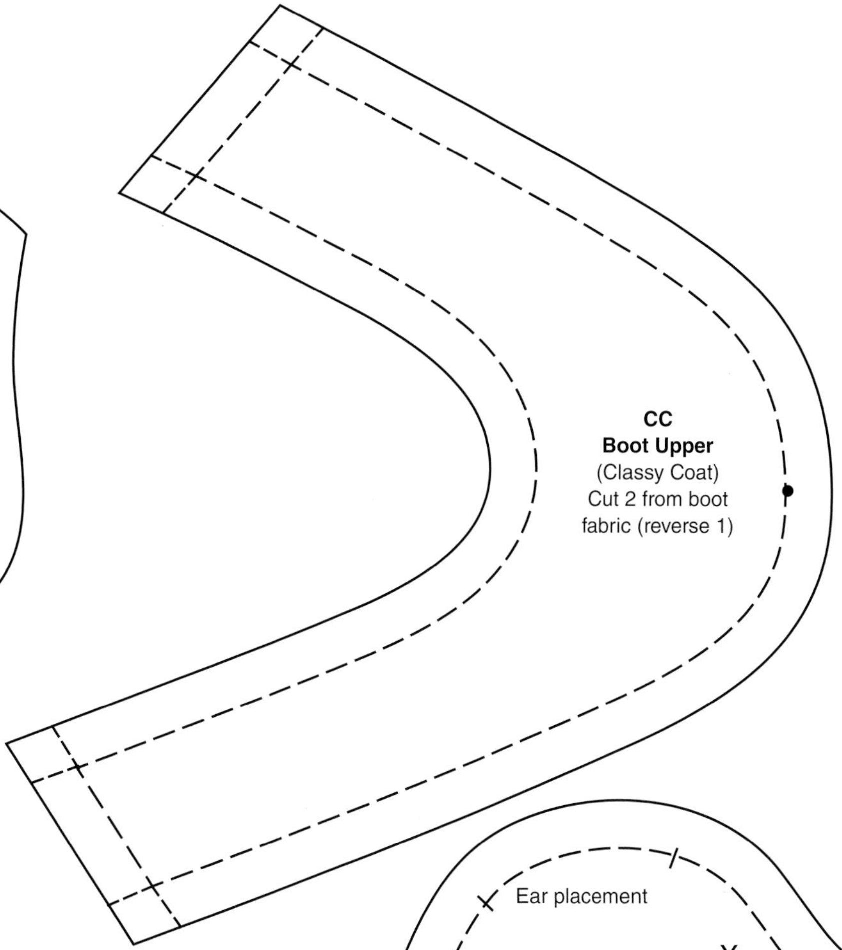

CC
Boot Upper
(Classy Coat)
Cut 2 from boot
fabric (reverse 1)

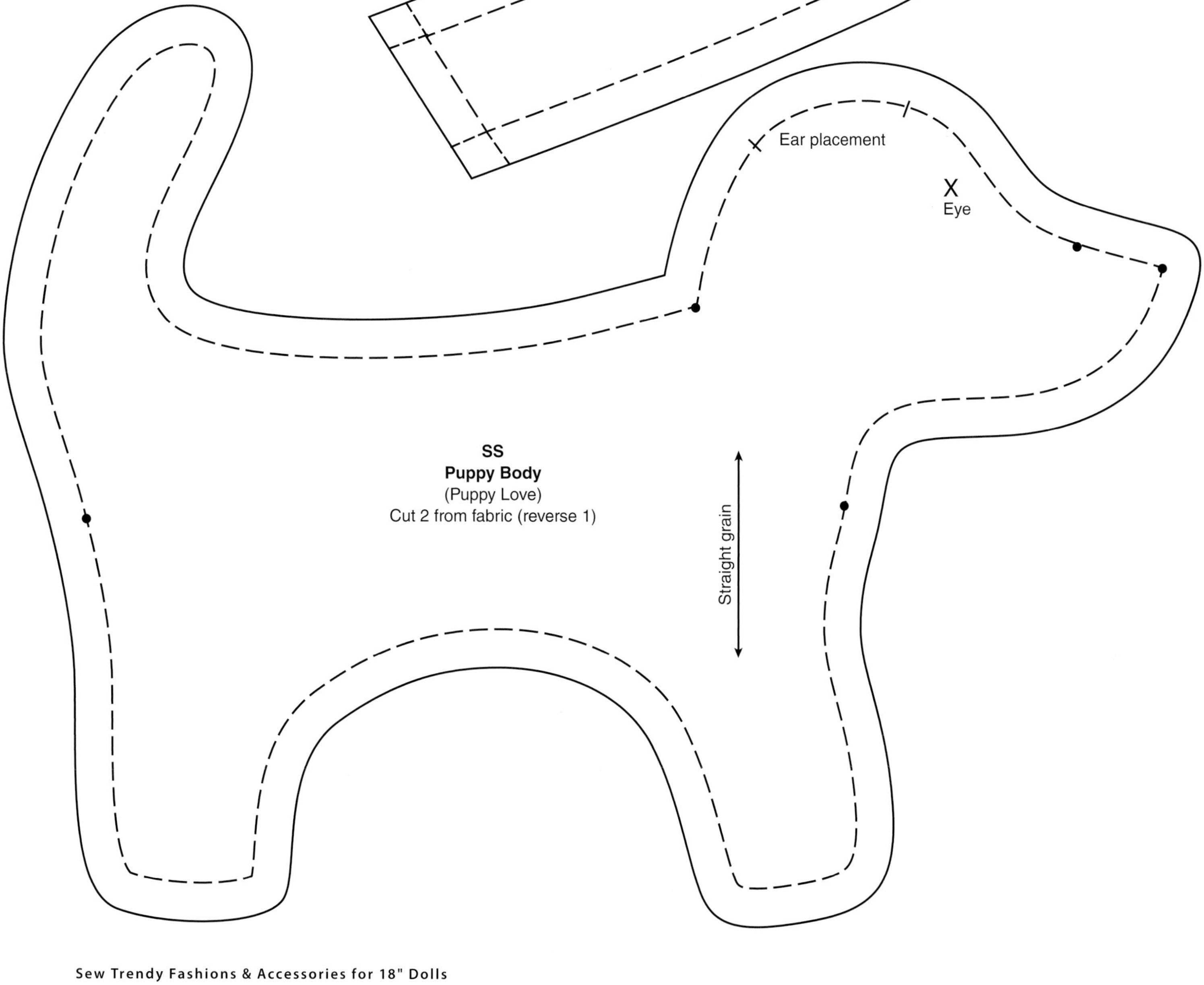

Ear placement

X
Eye

SS
Puppy Body
(Puppy Love)
Cut 2 from fabric (reverse 1)

Straight grain

Sew Trendy Fashions & Accessories for 18" Dolls

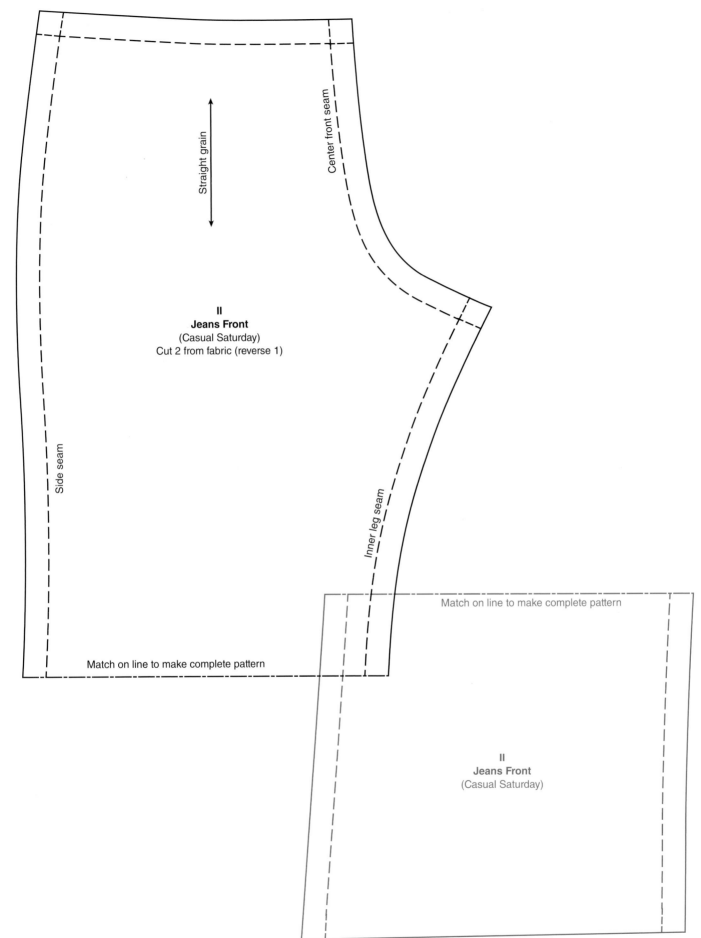

Straight grain

Center front seam

II
Jeans Front
(Casual Saturday)
Cut 2 from fabric (reverse 1)

Side seam

Inner leg seam

Match on line to make complete pattern

Match on line to make complete pattern

II
Jeans Front
(Casual Saturday)

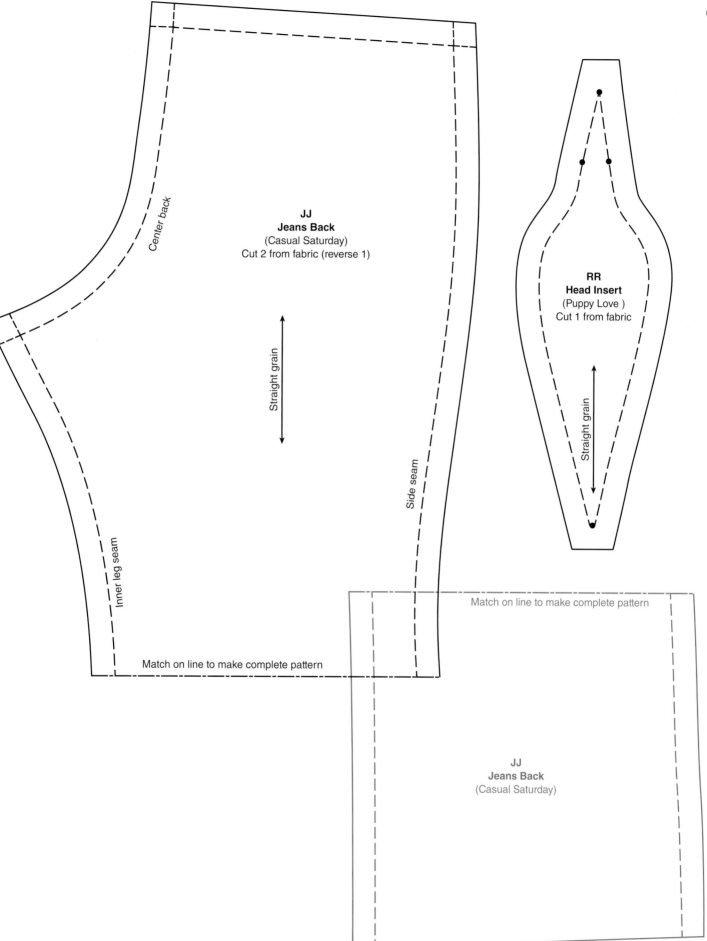

Center back

JJ
Jeans Back
(Casual Saturday)
Cut 2 from fabric (reverse 1)

Straight grain

RR
Head Insert
(Puppy Love)
Cut 1 from fabric

Straight grain

Side seam

Inner leg seam

Match on line to make complete pattern

Match on line to make complete pattern

JJ
Jeans Back
(Casual Saturday)

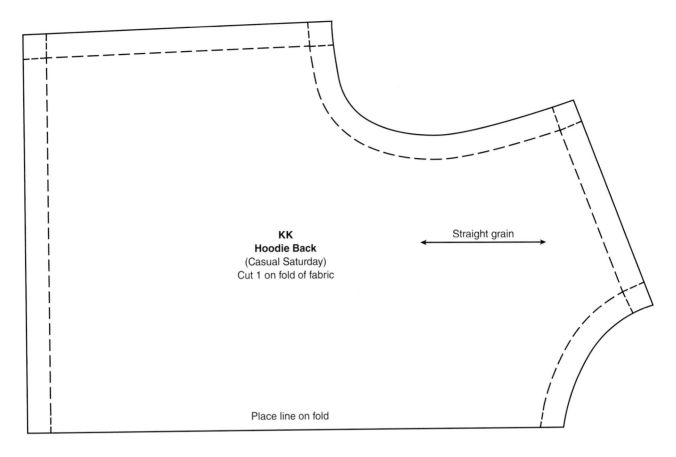

KK
Hoodie Back
(Casual Saturday)
Cut 1 on fold of fabric

Straight grain

Place line on fold

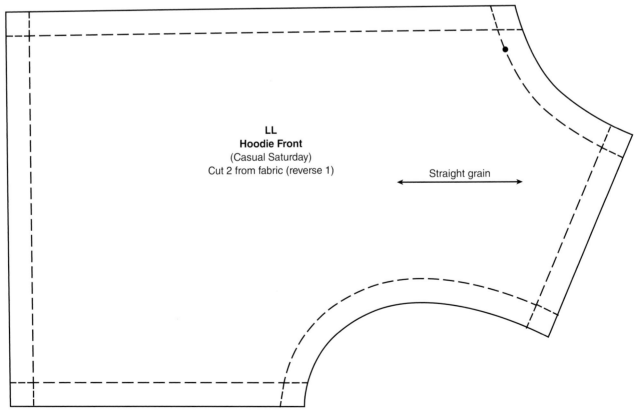

LL
Hoodie Front
(Casual Saturday)
Cut 2 from fabric (reverse 1)

Straight grain

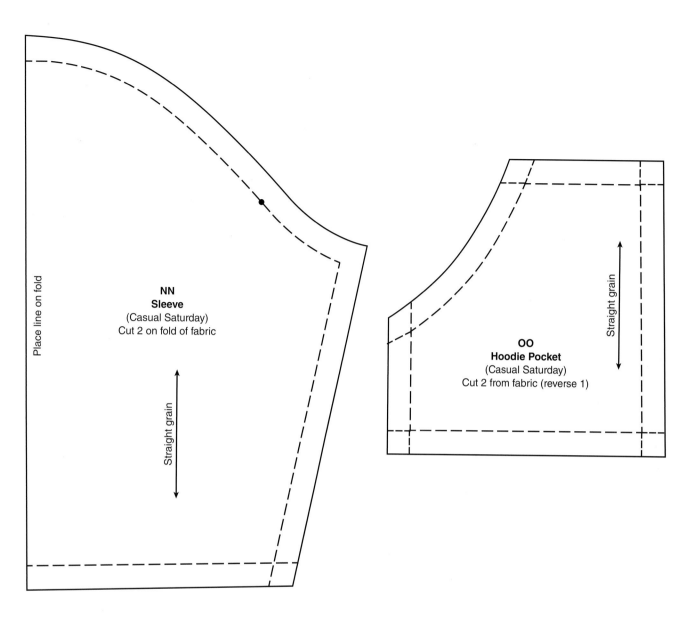

Place line on fold

NN
Sleeve
(Casual Saturday)
Cut 2 on fold of fabric

Straight grain

Straight grain

OO
Hoodie Pocket
(Casual Saturday)
Cut 2 from fabric (reverse 1)

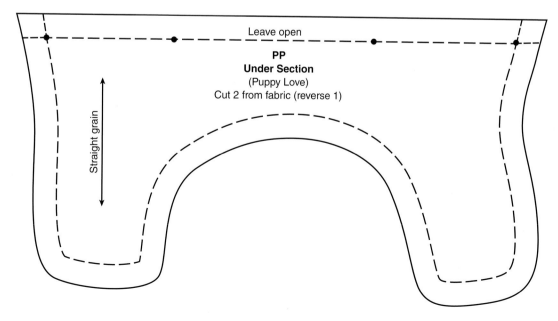

Leave open

PP
Under Section
(Puppy Love)
Cut 2 from fabric (reverse 1)

Straight grain

Photo Index

7

10

16

20

29

24

33

38

43

Annie's™ *Sew Trendy Fashions & Accessories* is published by Annie's, 306 East Parr Road, Berne, IN 46711. Printed in USA. Copyright © 2013 Annie's. All rights reserved. This publication may not be reproduced in part or in whole without written permission from the publisher.

RETAIL STORES: If you would like to carry this pattern book or any other Annie's publications, visit AnniesWSL.com

Every effort has been made to ensure that the instructions in this pattern book are complete and accurate. We cannot, however, take responsibility for human error, typographical mistakes or variations in individual work. Please visit AnniesCustomerCare.com to check for pattern updates.

ISBN: 978-1-59217-452-2

1 2 3 4 5 6 7 8 9